More Than MySpace

Recent Titles in
Libraries Unlimited Professional Guides for Young Adult Librarians
C. Allen Nichols and Mary Anne Nichols, Series Editors

Serving Homeschooled Teens and Their Parents
Maureen T. Lerch and Janet Welch

Reaching Out to Religious Youth: A Guide to Services, Programs, and Collections
L. Kay Carman

Classic Connections: Turning Teens on to Great Literature
Holly Koelling

Digital Inclusion, Teens, and Your Library: Exploring the Issues and Acting
on Them
Lesley S. J. Farmer

Extreme Teens: Library Services to Nontraditional Young Adults
Sheila B. Anderson

A Passion for Print: Promoting Reading and Books to Teens
Kristine Mahood

The Teen-Centered Book Club: Readers into Leaders
Bonnie Kunzel and Constance Hardesty

Teen Programs with Punch: A Month-by-Month Guide
Valerie A. Ott

Serving Young Teens and 'Tweens
Sheila B. Anderson, editor

The Guy-Friendly Teen Library: Serving Male Teens
Rollie Welch

Serving Urban Teens
Paula Brehm-Heeger

The Teen-Centered Writing Club: Bringing Teens and Words Together
Constance Hardesty

MORE THAN MYSPACE

Teens, Librarians, and Social Networking

Robyn M. Lupa, Editor

u Ottawa

Libraries Unlimited Professional Guides for Young
Adult Librarians
C. Allen Nichols and Mary Anne Nichols, Series Editors

LIBRARIES UNLIMITED
An Imprint of ABC-CLIO, LLC

A B C 🟰 C L I O

Santa Barbara, California • Denver, Colorado • Oxford, England

Library of Congress Cataloging-in-Publication Data

More than MySpace : teens, librarians, and social networking / Robyn M. Lupa,
editor.
        p. cm. — (Libraries Unlimited professional guides for young adult
librarians)
    Includes bibliographical references and index.
    ISBN 978-1-59158-760-6 (alk. paper)
1. Libraries and teenagers.   2. Internet in young adults' libraries.   3. Young
adults' libraries—Information technology.   4. Online social networks.
5. Technology and youth.   I. Lupa, Robyn M.
    Z718.5.M595   2009
    027.62'6—dc22   2009021373

13 12 11 10 09   1 2 3 4 5

This book is also available on the World Wide Web as an eBook.
Visit www.abc-clio.com for details.

ABC-CLIO, LLC
130 Cremona Drive, P.O. Box 1911
Santa Barbara, California 93116-1911

This book is printed on acid-free paper ∞
Manufactured in the United States of America

Copyright Acknowledgment

Excerpts from "Get Connected: Tech Programs for Teens" by Rosemary Honnold
for the Young Adult Library Services Association (YALSA and Neal-Schuman,
2007) are reprinted with permission.

CONTENTS

SERIES FOREWORD

We firmly believe that teens deserve equal access to library services, and that those services should equal to those offered to other library customers. This series supports that belief. We are proud of our association with Libraries Unlimited, which continues to prove itself as the premier publisher of books to help library staff serve teens. This series has succeeded because our authors know the needs of those library employees who work with young adults. Without exception, they have written useful and practical handbooks for library staff. We're glad to add Robyn Lupa to our list of authors.

Social networking has taken the world by storm, and in no more noticeable of a place, than in the lives of teens. Libraries are trying to adopt those technologies as a way of making ourselves more credible in the lives of the teens we serve, but what do they really mean for us? What kinds of programs and services can we offer utilizing these technologies? How can we teach teens to be safe using these technologies? This books shares answers to those questions and more.

We hope you find this book, as well as our entire series, to be informative, providing you with valuable ideas as you serve teens and that this work will further inspire you to do great things to make teens welcome in your library. If you have an idea for a title that could be added to our series, or would like to submit a book proposal, please email us at lu-books@ lu.com. We'd love to hear from you.

Mary Anne Nichols
C. Allen Nichols

ACKNOWLEDGMENTS

I would like to thank Sheila Mikkelson for ALA revelries and friendship and for encouraging me to pursue this exciting project. Thanks also to Larry Domingues of the Arvada Library in Jefferson County, Colorado, for his support through the years of my writing endeavors. I'm appreciative of my brother, Rob Lupa, for convincing me how appealing technology can be to kids and teens. Cheers to my girlfriends—Adrianne, Arra, Mary, Sandee, and Susan—for their support and participation in the indexing party. Finally, I am grateful to my friends on Facebook, which became an unexpectedly fun virtual getaway as I personally delved into the world of social networking.

INTRODUCTION: AVATARS, FRIENDS, APPS, OH MY! A BACKGROUND AND OVERVIEW

Robyn M. Lupa

WHAT IS SOCIAL NETWORKING?

No longer a new Internet technology buzzword, social networking has become a primary method by which people of all ages get to know each other and interact. In its broadest form, social networking can be described as making relevant ties between individuals based on specific types of interdependency. Online communities use social software to communicate within networks linked by friendship, similar pursuits, or comparable values. These virtual groups differ from the traditional definition of "community," which is limited to a specific geographical entity. In the online world, communities are fluid, with members coming and going and most likely involved in several simultaneously.

Today, Web sites and mobile applications allow visitors to personalize profiles of themselves and then participate in live chats, send e-mail, create content, and post comments. These all fall under the umbrella of social networking—Facebook, Twitter, MySpace, and Delicious (formerly Del. icio.us) may sound familiar! The world shrinks as people stay in constant contact with those deemed "friends." Friends may never meet face-to-face, yet they share common interests that compel them to follow or connect with one another. Friends are visible to others, and new connections can be made by simply asking. For example, you might ask to befriend your friend's friend. You can then communicate with each other via public comments on photos, videos, and blog entries or through private messages back and forth.

A BRIEF HISTORY OF SOCIAL NETWORKING

Since its inception on the World Wide Web, the universe of online social networking has evolved and become complex. We can trace its origins back to the Internet sites created to facilitate reconnection with lost school friends. Founded in 1995, Classmates.com (http://www.classmates.com) is credited as one of the pioneers, bringing together acquaintances from high school, college, the military, or past employment. From1997 to 2001, Six Degrees allowed people to create profiles and establish networks of friends and was the first to use the "web of contacts" model of social networking (Brown, 1998). Friendster (http://www.friendster.com) was created in 2002 as a way to establish and cultivate general friendships (rather than the limited universe of former classmates). Friendster allows users to visualize how social connections are made, make plans with each other, and forge new ties. In 1999, blogging software became available, enabling users to share their lives with the world through online diaries. LiveJournal and Blogger were among the first. By 2008, over 112 million blogs were being tracked (Helmond, 2008).

In 2004, MySpace (http://www.myspace.com) emerged to provide a social network for unsigned musicians. It featured a range of music connections, space for specific bands, and space for fans of these bands. Within two years, it was the most popular site in the United States (Tancer, 2006). MySpace especially appealed to its audience because it included the capability to customize their pages with graphics, pictures, and eventually videos and other fun applications. For teens this was like decorating their bedrooms and inviting friends to hang out—with even greater potential for individualistic expression. Facebook (http://www.facebook.com) emerged around the same time with a completely different look and capabilities to find and interact with friends.

TODAY'S SOCIAL NETWORKING ENVIRONMENT

An explosion of online social interactivity has since enabled users to share literary efforts, music, pictures, videos, and life interests for fun, business networking, consumerism, politics, promotion, and marketing. This phenomenon is part of the growth of Web 2.0, the second generation of the World Wide Web, allowing for virtual collaboration via blogs, wikis, podcasting, tagging, and more. Web 2.0 has changed how we use the Internet in a multitude of ways. Consider the possibilities suggested in the following samplings.

POLITICS AND ACTIVISM

- Students involved in the When History Happens learning community (http://www.whenhistoryhappens.org) shared immediate firsthand experiences from the floors of the 2008 Democratic and Republican National Conventions by texting and blogging to followers.

- The 2008 presidential candidates reached out to millions of Facebook users with incentives to become supporters of their official sites, to view live video of events, and to include applications on profile pages that displayed the candidate's virtual yard signs. Facebook subscribers were invited to join groups such as "Librarians Against Sarah Palin" or "Young People Against Barack Obama for President"; to register for an early/absentee ballot; and to watch and then comment on candidate's TV ads.

- Politicians adopted MySpace and YouTube as forums to describe their positions on issues, impart biographical information and visual introductions, post videos of speeches and interviews, and interact with pop culture figures (http://www.youtube.com/you choose).

- Young people find out about how to volunteer and get involved in social causes via MTVs "Just Cause" activism program (http://www.mtv.com/thinkmtv/research/pdf/Just.Cause.FNL.APX.pdf). With the premise that "community" has been redefined, the Internet becomes a primary tool to promote social change.

PROFESSIONAL NETWORKING AND RESOURCES

- Businesses and special interest groups have also adopted technology to share information. Professionals build relationships based on education and career paths, write recommendations for each other, form new connections through old ones, and learn about job opportunities at companies within distinctive networks. For example, LinkedIn (http://www.linkedin.com) provides an avenue for business professionals to interact with one another.

- Librarians involved on Facebook can join groups named "Librarians and Facebook," "Library 2.0 Interest Group," and "American Library Association Members"; and you can become a fan of the Young Adult Library Services Association (YALSA) by joining its page (http://www.facebook.com/pages/YALSA/35222707784).

- Many librarians and other interested parties also follow Pop Goes the Library (http://www.popgoesthelibrary.com), which advocates the recognition of pop culture by librarians and contains contributions from notable names in the field. Subscribers read about book display possibilities, get alerts on nostalgic TV shows that are now available on DVD, and discover reviews of new movie releases that patrons will be talking about.

- Interactive Web sites, called Wikis, allow you to collaborate online and create as a group. Users can edit and expand on content created by others. YALSA's wiki (http://wikis.ala.org/yalsa/index.php/Main_Page) allows teen librarians to monitor—and contribute to—news and valuable resources.

CURRENT EVENTS

- National Public Radio listeners can now get their news from traditional radio broadcasts, from NPR's Web site, and from topical podcasts (http://www.npr.org/rss/podcast/podcast_directory.php). The latest episode may be listened to on a laptop or downloaded onto an MP3 player. Audience members may also opt to subscribe to and receive only specific programs—for example, you may subscribe to every episode of "All Songs Considered," "Car Talk's Call of the Week," "Children's Literature with Daniel Pinkwater," "Talk of the Nation," or "Sunday Puzzle."

- Other news sites, such as USA TODAY (http://www.usatoday.com), allow readers to become members of its community and engage in stories.

RECREATIONAL INTERESTS AND CONSUMERISM

- Vlog (video blog) fans watch video clips to learn how to cook, experience virtual travel, enjoy snippets from local music festivals, watch a long-distance relative's birthday party, and even taste wine (http://tv.winelibrary.com). You can then post comments on the vlog site, beginning a dialogue that may lead to new connections with other people who are also following the videos.

- MP3 owners download podcasts to listen to everything from news stories to book reviews, fitness programs, and guided meditation. Stanford University allows iTunes users to download faculty lectures, interviews, and courses in the form of podcasts (http://itunes.stanford.edu).

- Lala (http://www.lala.com), a music-sharing site, offers you the capability to listen to and download songs while connecting online with real people to share playlists, recommend new tunes, and discuss common musical interests.

- Amazon (http://www.amazon.com) has become much more than an online shopping source. Before making a purchase, customers can now browse reviews from others and, once the product is in hand, comment on or rate it themselves.

SOCIALIZING AND JOURNALING

- Vox (http://www.vox.com), another blogging service, features pictures, video, audio files, and text pages designed around a personal style. It encourages you to establish your own "online neighborhood" in order to share life experiences.

- Diaries are no longer private. LiveJournal (http://www.livejournal.com) bloggers post their innermost ramblings, commentaries, observations, daily habits, and confessionals for user-defined networks to read and then respond to and form an ongoing dialogue.

- Orkut's (http://www.orkut.com) international community operates under defined standards in order to make your social life "more active and stimulating."

- In Second Life (http://www.SecondLife.com), a virtual reality site, users create 3-D personas (avatars) and interact with each other in worlds that echo the physical one. Second Life mirrors real life to the extent that property and merchandise may be purchased. Avatars communicate by chatting online, playing games, or attending events. Those lacking real-world social confidence have the opportunity to come out of their shell—you may choose to be an avatar that has no resemblance to your mortal self. A quiet, geeky guy can be a superhero or Jedi. A normally timid girl can be a supermodel or martial arts expert. You might even select an animal to represent yourself. Some university libraries have established islands in Second Life, where they work with educators to expand this new literacy. Students meet there for job fairs, technology training, lectures, and demonstrations; ask questions at the reference desk; and attend book discussions.

- Moblogging (mobile-blogging) software enables you to update online blogs via voice or texting from cell phones. Camera phones allow for images to be uploaded remotely. Twitter (http://www.twitter.com) asks a simple question, "What are you doing?" In 140 characters or less, you can send friends "tweets"—very short updates—throughout the day. Individually, these don't amount to much. Collectively, though, they provide a rich picture of someone's day-to-day activities and thoughts.

SURFING AND SHARING

- Sites such as Digg (http://www.digg.com) have evolved as opportunities for people to make interesting and unique Web discoveries. Communities of users submit sites for others to discover and give opinions on, ultimately hoping the sites will be featured on Digg.

- StumbleUpon (http://www.stumbleupon.com) asks you to define your likes and then "channelsurfs" the Internet to recommend relevant sites and encourages connections among people who have similar interests.

- Delicious (http://www.delicious.com) is called a "social bookmarking site." It allows you not only to organize favorite Web sites but to do so in a novel approach that is more powerful than traditional folders. Bookmarked sites are shared with others within a community. For example, on its teen Web page, the Nashville Public Library features links on such topics as manga, getting social help, careers, and homework (http://www.delicious.com/nashpubya).

- Established back in 1999, Cyworld (http://us.cyworld.com) gives you yet another way to connect, by creating a "mini-room" that can be decorated with animated backgrounds, appliances, furniture and animated friends, and even a "mini-me." Within the site, users can join clubs that reflect their interests, such as "I Love Math!" "I Love Starbucks!" and "High School Musical Rules!"

- Social networking also appeals to preteens and even younger children, with sites such as Whyville, AllyKatzz, Club Penguin, Cartoon Doll Emporium, Habbo Hotel, Webkinz, WeeWorld, Stardoll, and BarbieGirls.com. These interactive play spaces and animated worlds offer safe places to hang out with friends and chat about interests and are an opportunity for safe self-expression. Messages are filtered and/or monitored, and no personal information may be shared. Primarily these sites are free to use, but parents may pay a small fee ($5–8/month) for premium access and full features.

- At Flickr (http://www.flickr.com), a photo-sharing site, you can make friends, give feedback on pictures, and share them among designated contacts.
- YouTube (http://www.youtube.com) operates similarly, with videos rather than still pictures.

WHAT IS SOCIAL NETWORKING'S CULTURAL RELEVANCE?

In *The Great Good Place*, Ray Oldenburg (1989) laments that good human relations were not fostered within the structure of our urban, industrialized society. With compartmentalization and a lack of public meeting places, individuals were ignorant of the interests of those not in their own immediate social group. People who transported themselves back and forth from work to home and back to work lacked community. Mental health, Oldenburg (2008) contends, and affirmative socialization depend on the existence of community within our lives.

Online technology may be viewed as a solution to this disconnect. Before ARPANET, the early incarnation of the internet, went online in 1969, J.C.R. Licklider and Robert W. Taylor (1968) wrote an article titled "The Computer as a Communication Device." Having sponsored the Internet's initial development, they set forth their vision for the future of computer-linked communities, predicting that people would ultimately be able to communicate more effectively via computers than face-to-face:

> And we believe that we are entering a technological age in which we will be able to interact with the richness of living information— not merely in the passive way that we have become accustomed to using books and libraries, but as active participants in an ongoing process, bringing something to it through our interaction with it, and not simply receiving something from it by our connection to it.

The very idea of passive libraries? By embracing social networking, we can change that perception—read on!

Oldenburg (1989) proposes three essential places in people's lives: the place we live, the place we work, and the place we gather for conviviality. Although the casual conversation that takes place in cafes, beauty shops, pubs, and town squares is universally considered to be trivial talk, Oldenburg makes the case that such places are where communities can come into being and continue to hold together. People have a need to belong. We have our families; we have our interactions at school, at work, and at places of worship; we join clubs and civic organizations. Now, with technology, the concept of "community" extends to the whole world, where connections are made specifically because of common interests. Just as regulars at Starbucks greet each other over lattes, exchange brief conversations and updates, and discuss the morning headlines, so do members of virtual communities who check in with one another often.

Trent Batson (2008) wrote in "The Social Web: Academic Zoning Rules,"

> The social Web is an outward sign of an inner human social reality and drive. And it works well, surprisingly well. Good social sites can serve to remind you of friends you knew long ago or colleagues you've lost touch with. They support a new, or very old, human conversation, so we know what those in our "small town on the Web" are doing, how to get a hold of them from anywhere in the world, and remind you of their title or of their own group of colleagues—as part of a *conversation* instead of a Web search.

The beauty of social networking is precisely as Batson describes—it has taken the vast and overwhelming World Wide Web and shrunk it into a small community for those who opt to tap in. Search YouTube for the video "Social Media in Plain English" (LeFever, 2008) for a humorous, yet informative explanation of this concept.

Clearly the realm of electronic correspondence between people has become a greater phenomenon than sharing e-mails and individual Web sites. In every niche imaginable, people connect, discuss, relate, assist, and advise. As Harold Rheingold (1998) observed, virtual communities form "when people carry on public discussions long enough, with *sufficient human feeling*, to form webs of personal relationships." Based on the examples cited earlier, this mode of relating to one another is our new reality.

HOW IS SOCIAL NETWORKING USED BY TEENS?

Various labels have been applied to children born after 1980, including the N (Net)-Gen, the D (Digital)-Gen, and Digital Natives (Prensky, 2001). Regardless of their moniker, we can find certain commonalities across this broad age group. A great many of today's students grew up with digital technology for entertainment, communication, and education. Those who lack that exposure will likely be behind their peers academically and, later, in the workforce. (That's where libraries can help.) Although not all are computer owners or avid users of the technology, they have spent their entire lives exposed to and even surrounded by computers, video games, cameras that produce both photos and video, cell phones that enable much more than two-way conversations, and iPods. Digital media is so integrated in the lives of today's teens that they even think differently from us. They process information differently than we do and apply the tools in different ways than we do. Students know that they can use the Internet to learn about any topic. And many know that they can easily connect with others online for multiple reasons—from roaming around as a cartoon penguin to announcing parties and events to working together virtually on math homework. Students are now entering higher education with new expectations regarding technology in support of learning and they refer to these technologies as being resources that must adapt to the student's needs (Oblinger, 2005).

MySpace and Facebook have become the hangouts for this generation. They enable users to define and express themselves by joining and contributing to political and activist groups. Personal popularity may be demonstrated through lists of friends, and levels of communication with those friends range from intimate to very casual interactions. Teens can remain in close contact with anyone, anywhere. The concept of a long-distance phone call is meaningless to them. E-mail, instant messaging, and moblogging have allowed online-only friendships to evolve.

Technology has not altered the broad developmental phases of adolescence. Teens still experience the need to establish a peer group, acquire social skills, and seek an individual identity. However, the landscape in which this is being done is shifting. Teens now have the means to find and define themselves, as well as to make and interact with friends digitally.

In her presentation "Social Media and Libraries: New Applications for a New Generation of Users," Mary Madden (2007) remarked that "teenagers are increasingly becoming library immigrants in a land of library natives." "MySpace," she wrote, "might seem chaotic...But it offers a stable sense of place in the midst of drastic social changes that happen during the teenage years...Teens know that ordinary citizens can be publishers, movie makers, artists, song creators, and storytellers. 57% of online teens have created some kind of content for the Internet."

Clearly, the "social Web" is well established among youth.

HOW DOES THIS APPLY TO
PUBLIC LIBRARIES?

You may be wondering what all this has to do with you as a librarian. Embrace the technology! In *The Virtual Community*, Rheingold (1998) writes that the experience of online neighborhoods is conveyed by graphic imagery and the sense of place they offer to you. However, a biological analogy may be more appropriate to describe the way cyberculture has changed over the years: "In terms of the way the whole system is propagating and evolving, think of cyberspace as a social petri dish, the Net as the agar medium and virtual communities, in all their diversity, as the colonies of microorganisms that grow in petri dishes. Each of the small colonies of microorganisms—the communities on the Net—is a social experiment that nobody planned but that is happening nevertheless." The public library is unique in that it is a real civic space that allows its users to socialize both in person and virtually for free.

Social networking may also be compared to Oldenburg's third place, when applied to libraries that embrace it to reach patrons. The first is the physical building and its outlets (kiosks, bookmobiles); the second is the online environment of the library's Web site. The third is similar to the first—where patrons can actually interact with the library, but in a virtual space. The distinction between using simple online communication and participating in online communities is most exemplified by teen's use of the technology. Lurk in any public library today, and you will inevitably discover teens as the primary users of social networking tools. They may be glued to a keyboard and monitor, but they are interacting with dozens of people during their online sessions.

The concept of social media ties directly into another buzzword, New Literacies. In October 2008, the American Association of School Libraries revamped their *Standards for the 21st Century Learner*, in response to input from AASL members. This important document acknowledges that digitization and technological tools have changed learning. Students are expected to use technology to access quality information and to make sense of it, draw conclusions from it, and share knowledge. Communication may be through video, music, virtual worlds, games, and photos as well as print materials. With these new standards, school librarians are making the commitment to acknowledge the new learning landscape—not limited to the K–12 years, but as a foundation for the rest of students' lives.

College students are now required to subscribe to electronic discussion lists and participate in academic forums that take place on blogs and wikis. Christopher Jennings (2008), assistant professor of technical communications and media production at the Metropolitan State College of Denver, comments,

> Blogs, wikis and, to an extent, social networking platforms illustrate the various ways in which students reflect on their very recent experiences by collaborating within an online e-learning environment. Wikis, fully editable websites, are easily accessible, require no software and allow its contributors—in this case, students—to feel a sense of responsibility and ownership. Wikis are everywhere as research tools, and industries are using them for project management collaboration. It is our responsibility as professors to provide opportunities for students to gain experience using technologies that are applicable to everyday life. This includes social and professional means by which our students communicate and are expected to know upon graduation. Libraries can help by providing access to these technologies as learning tools, learning environments, research mechanisms, and social collaboration.

The cover of October 2007's *American Libraries* features a teen holding up a cell phone with the caption "It's All About Books—Not! Teens and the New Literacy." In the article, author Michael Cart (2007) begins with statistics on the decline of pleasure reading among young adults. He challenges these statistics by asking readers to define "reading." Audio books, Web sites, blogs, wikis, and online communication all should qualify. While education experts lament declining reading rates and scores among teens, some librarians and YA authors are responding with, "Define reading!" Some argue that technology-based "reading" should be acknowledged and accepted by adults and, consequently, given validity for the teens who engage in it. Along the same line, renowned teen author David Levithan credits social networking—being able to communicate excitement about books and easily interact with authors who have an online presence—with inspiring a boom in YA publishing! (Reno, 2008)

Consider what the younger kids—tweens—are doing in your library today. Many have accounts on ClubPenguin and Webkinz. Some e-mail Grandma their thanks for their birthday package, rather than using a stamp to convey that appreciation. Many download tunes for their own MP3 players. Most would say with confidence that they can answer any question by Googling it. As one 10-year-old recently remarked, "There's a dot com for everything!" Now think about how these kids will, in a few years, become your teen patron base.

In 2005, 87 percent of U.S. teens aged 12–17 used the Internet, and 51 percent of teenage users said they went online on a daily basis. Teens are also using instant messaging for longer periods of time. On a typical day, the largest group of teens (37%) say they instant-message (IM) for a half hour to an hour. One-quarter (27%) say they IM for less than a half hour a day, and another quarter (24%) say they IM for one to two hours a day. The average teen IMs with 35 people for three hours a week (National Labor Committee, 2006). Those stats are a few years old—how much has usage grown by now?

Let's look back at the lofty goals for social networking set by Licklider and Taylor (1968) a few decades ago:

> If the network idea should prove to do for education what a few have envisioned in hope, if not in concrete detailed plan, and if all minds should prove to be responsive, surely the boon to humankind would be beyond measure.

By seizing the opportunity to understand and apply social networking tools that are already a part of teens' social and academic lives, libraries can and will make an impact. Keep in mind that growing up with digital media does not ensure kids are using it safely, wisely, and in full capacity as information tools. The American Library Association (2007) agrees: "Learning to use today's Internet, and specifically interactive web applications...is now an essential component of education, as these learning and social environments are promoted more and more. The development of information literacy skills requires that young people be able to safely and effectively use these important new collaborative tools." If we step up to educate teens on the benefits and savvy use of social networking, they will be more apt to become habitual library users. Basic marketing, selling the library to this demographic, and becoming that boon to humankind is not something we can afford to forego. Libraries offer a safe place to use these tools responsibly. Marcellus Turner (2008), executive director of the Jefferson County Public Library in Colorado, makes this assertion:

> It is a given that libraries are changing. Generation Y users and technology are changing us. We will always be relied on to bridge the digital divide. Where will libraries be in five years? I don't know...the technology is changing every day, and a lot can happen. But I do

know that we have to change with it in order to remain relevant to our users. And let's enjoy this with our community; let's have a good time with this partnership—rather than simply just doing it!

WHAT IS THE PURPOSE OF THIS BOOK?

This book focuses on the use of virtual communities by teenagers and on what public libraries can and should do to support them. We begin with Dave Moyer, a dynamic high school student who has observed the rising popularity of social networking among his peers. Public library/school liaison Erin Downey Howerton explores the power and appeal of social networking to teens and shares her cautions and concerns. A teacher with her pulse on 21st-century learning, Michelle Pearson, gives her perspective on how crucial it is for educators—and librarians—to advocate and collaborate on new technologies. Dedicated teen librarian Jenna Obee gives you an overview of top social networking sites as they apply to public libraries, tips on how to put them to good use, and real-world examples. Technology guru Kelly Czarnecki explains why public libraries cannot ignore the social networking phenomenon and discusses precisely how to safely get on board. Now fully immersed in social networking, I give you some ideas on how you and your teen patrons can have fun with it. Progressive librarian Andrew Wilson describes an exciting initiative to market the online homework resources of the New York City libraries directly to kids. Next, Linda Braun, an advocate for information literacy, tells us why involvement in social networking is professionally advantageous. Finally, after recapping a survey of social networking usage that I conducted with public librarians, I offer you a 2.0 challenge!

WORKS CITED

American Association of School Libraries. 2008. *AASL Standards for the 21st-Century Learner.* http://www.ala.org/ala/mgrps/divs/aasl/guidelinesandstan dards/learningstandards/standards.cfm (accessed May 20, 2009).

American Library Association. 2007. *Interactive Web Applications.* http://wikis.ala. org/iwa/index.php/Main_Page (accessed May 20, 2009).

Batson, Trent. 2008. "The social web: Academic zoning rules." *Campus Technology,* April 16. http://campustechnology.com/articles/60934 (accessed May 20, 2009).

Brown, Janelle. 1998. "Six degrees to nowhere." *Salon,* September 21. http://archive. salon.com/21st/reviews/1998/09/21review.html (accessed June 1, 2009).

Cart, Michael. 2007. "It's all about books—not! Teens and the new literacy." *American Libraries* 38 (9): 52–54.

Helmond, Anne. 2008. "How many blogs are there? Is someone still counting?" *Blog Herald*, February 11. http://www.blogherald.com/2008/02/11/how-many-blogs-are-there-is-someone-still-counting (accessed May 20, 2009).

Jennings, Christopher. 2008. Interview by Robyn Lupa, March 15.

LeFever, Lee. 2008. "Social media in plain English." *Common Craft*, May 29. http://www.commoncraft.com/socialmedia (accessed May 20, 2009).

Licklider, J.C.R., and Robert W. Taylor. 1968. "The computer as communication device." http://www.kurzweilai.net/meme/frame.html?main=/articles/art0353.html (accessed May 22, 2009).

Madden, Mary. 2007. *Social Media and Libraries: New Applications for a New Generation of Users.* http://www.pewinternet.org/PPF/r/92/presentation_display.asp (accessed May 22, 2009).

National Labor Committee. 2006. *How U.S. Teens Spend Their Time and Money.* http://www.nlcnet.org/article.php?id=220 (accessed May 22, 2009).

Oblinger, D. and J. Oblinger. 2005. *Educating the Net Generation.* http://www.educause.edu/educatingthenetgen (accessed June 2, 2009).

Oldenburg, Ray. 1989. *The Great Good Place: Cafes, Coffee Shops, Community Centers, Beauty Parlors, General Stores, Bars, Hangouts, and How They Get You through the Day.* New York: Paragon House, 1989.

Oldenburg, Ray. 2008. *Project for Public Spaces.* http://www.pps.org/info/placemakingtools/placemakers/roldenburg#quotable (accessed May 22, 2009).

Prensky, Marc. 2001. *Digital Natives, Digital Immigrants.* http://www.twitchspeed.com/site/Prensky%20-%20Digital%20Natives,%20Digital%20Immigrants%20-%20Part1.htm (accessed May 22, 2009).

Reno, Jamie. 2008. "Generation R (R is for reader)." *Newsweek*, May 14. http://www.newsweek.com/id/136961?tid=relatedcl (accessed May 22, 2009).

Rheingold, Howard. 1998. *The Virtual Community.* http://www.rheingold.com/vc/book/index.html (accessed May 22, 2009).

Tancer, Bill. 2006. "MySpace Moves Into #1 Position for All Internet Sites." *Hitwise*, July 11. http://weblogs.hitwise.com/bill-tancer/2006/07/myspace_moves_into_1_position.html (accessed May 20, 20009).

Turner, Marcellus. 2008. Interview by Robyn Lupa, October 27.

1

◇ ◇ ◇

WORDS FROM THE WIRED: A TEEN PERSPECTIVE

Dave Moyer

Not even five years ago, a great amount of a teenager's time after school was spent on the phone. "Did you hear what happened with Ashton and Alexis?" "I know! They were so perfect together!" A parent might hope their cell phone plan had unlimited minutes or that their child was making a local call on their constantly tied-up landline. If not, their teenager's everyday social life would rack up a bill more expensive than the annual tab for a private jet plane. Parents constantly nagged their young chatterboxes to do their homework or spend some time with the *family* for a change and warned that if they kept hanging their head over the side of the bed like that, they would get permanent brain damage!

This situation is nothing new. Part of growing up is talking (a lot), no matter how or where. Before the age of the telephone, it would be rare for a mother to see her teenager without at least one friend, desperate to continue conversations once the school day had ended. Then, when they couldn't chat in person, elaborate systems of tin cans and strings graced the neighborhood skyline (because Nancy absolutely needed to know all about that one boy in Christina's chemistry class right away). Now, in the advent of the digital age, the youth of the world have moved on to a new way of staying connected: the Internet. Even four years ago, I remember the daily after-school chatter transitioning from "call me tonight" to "I'll be on MySpace!" The concept is the same—many parents now complain about how their kids spend hours on the computer, completely disconnected from those around them! The story never changes, just the technology behind it.

In 2003, a company called eUniverse decided they were going to get in on this hip, new "social networking" thing that was becoming so popular with the college crowd. Within 10 days, the Internet saw the very first version of MySpace. Initially targeting music fans, the site was an instant hit, reaching a massive 30 percent of the 170 million people with Internet access by May 2006 (comScore, 2006a). However, a strange trend started to emerge from MySpace's statistics: the percentage of users ages 12 to 17 began growing at a surprisingly quick rate! Leading Internet analyst comScore revealed that by August 2006, nearly 12 percent of unique visitors to MySpace were in that oddly young demographic (comScore, 2006b).

These kids were smart, setting up their own profiles and blogs and finding all of their friends rather quickly. Though MySpace supposedly stopped users under age 13 from joining the site, a fake birthday was just a click away, and soon sparkling hearts and pictures taken in the bathroom mirror graced profiles of people "99 years old" hailing from "Zimbabwe." Messages were zapped back and forth all night long, blog posts (though short and unstructured) were written, and "lols" were typed. Soon, the use of phones began to decrease. The number of rollover minutes on cell phone plans slowly went up. Kids were moving online and taking their conversations with them. Social networking has even started to work its way into offline discussion. It is fairly common to hear a teenager describe a picture just taken on his cell phone as a "total MySpace picture," perfect to use as post on his profile on a favorite social networking service.

In 2004, after merely a week of development, a Harvard student named Mark Zuckerberg launched a Web site for social interactions exclusive to Harvard. He stated that he wanted to be the first to create what many had asked for: a "universal face book for the school." Mark called the site thefacebook.com, and its numbers quickly grew into the thousands (Tabak, 2004).

By March of that year, the site had been extended to other high-profile universities such as Yale and Stanford. Soon high school and employer networks were added, and the site, now called simply Facebook, had numbers in the millions (Facebook, 2008).

Finally, with millions of dollars of funding in the bag, Facebook's management decided that it was time to get in on that wide-open demographic contributing to the success of sites such as MySpace. The company announced that it was opening its doors to absolutely anyone in September 2006 (Hansell, 2006), and many junior high students and highschoolers instantly took to the service. It was just one more example of the ground that kids were and are gaining in social networking.

Facebook also introduced an exciting new feature to online life that made it even more appealing: the ability to add "applications" to your profile, with surveys, quizzes, fun videos, and games to simply display or play with your friends. A simple log-on to the Facebook profile of an average teenager will more than likely yield a plethora of invitations to see what kind of muffin you really are or find what movie star you are most like. Maybe someone threw a cow at you, and you need to throw a cow back, or maybe you have just been nominated by a friend as their very best friend on Facebook (along with hundreds of other friends they are connected to).

In the younger age group, many people seem to be in a race of sorts, trying to gain as many "friends" as possible. With lots of teens their list of "friends" online is by no means exclusive to friends in real life. When I first got on MySpace three years ago, I remember getting a friend request from someone who would never even get near me away from the computer! In essence, the number of friends you have on your profile is a symbol of social status for many teens. The more friends a person has, the more popular she is in real life, right? The average profile of a middleschooler often has a friend counter of over 500 or, increasingly often, in the thousands! You do not even need to have heard of someone once before; you just add them as a friend. Katy Perry has a MySpace? Add her! The idea seems to be the more, the merrier, when it comes to the Net.

Technology is revolutionizing every single aspect of our daily lives. From coffee makers to cars, the 21st century is changing the world, and our social interactions are no exception. Though tin cans and strings now seem infinitely obsolete when compared to today's fiber-optic data lines, the need to interact is just as strong as it was before. As we enter the digital age, we have the ability to have conversations with people we have never even met, while sharing photos, videos, and music at speeds that just 10 years ago were thought impossible. From posting a comment on a friend's page to having a snowball fight with hundreds of "friends" for months, social networking is changing the way that people live their lives, no matter what their age.

WORKS CITED

comScore. 2006a. *More Than Half of MySpace Visitors Are Now Age 35 or Older, as the Site's Demographic Composition Continues to Shift.* http://www.comscore.com/Press_Events/Press_Releases/2006/10/More_than_Half_MySpace_Visitors_Age_35/(language)/eng-US accessed May 22, 2009).

comScore. 2006b. *Social Networking Sites Continue to Attract Record Numbers as MySpace.com Surpasses 50 Million U.S. Visitors in May.* http http://comscore.com/Press_Events/Press_Releases/2006/06/MySpace_Surpasses_50_Million_Visitors/(language)/eng-US accessed May 22, 2009).

Facebook. 2008. *Company Timeline.* http://www.facebook.com/press/info.php?timeline (accessed May 22, 2009).

Hansell, Saul. 2006. "Site previously for students will be opened up to others." *New York Times,* September 12. http://www.nytimes.com/2006/09/12/technology/12online.html?_r=1&oref=slogin (accessed May 22, 2009).

Tabak, Alan J. 2004. "Hundreds register for new Facebook website." *The Harvard Crimson,* February 9. http://www.thecrimson.com/article.aspx?ref=357292 (accessed May 22, 2009).

2

◇ ◇ ◇

FRIENDS, FUN, FADS—AND FEAR: TEENS IN THE 21ST CENTURY

Erin Downey Howerton

Web 2.0 and social networking have provided today's teenagers with a new place to gather, as well as a new vocabulary. For example, the word "friend" can now be a noun or a verb. When someone is "friended" or "defriended," these actions play out in front of a larger audience on social networking Web sites. The phenomenon of social networking is commonly said to have been made possible by Web 2.0, or the "social Web." Once Web sites introduced interaction and customization on sites that formerly you could consume only passively, the online world shifted. The participatory Web is a world of potential connections waiting to be made, and teens are acutely aware of and tapped into this network.

Social networks' teen appeal happened for several reasons—the online space reflects real life, and in real life, social interactions are highly important to teens, providing them a way to make sense of the world (boyd, 2006). Also, as real-world space has increasingly contracted for teens, they have moved online to take advantage of the medium and its power to connect. Additionally, online spaces are foreign to many parents and other adults, making it attractive to youth culture. Each generation desires to make their mark on the world and reject old patterns of behavior. As rock and roll was for the boomers, so too is social networking for Gen Y and Millennials.

Of course, this brave new digital world is not without controversy. The easily made social bonds can stretch and break under the weight of cyber-bullying; an admirer can become a cyberstalker; and the hype fuels hysteria with a morphed sort of "stranger danger." The predator script looms large in modern media as an omnipresent threat that can enter homes relatively unseen through these networks. Pictures or words posted as a lark one day can haunt teens the next when a school or an employer checks their profile.

Despite the highs and lows of social networking, teens have managed to make this silicon frontier their own land rush; they are pioneers in an adolescence mediated via a screen. And although social networks may reflect much of the offline world, they may also be creating new habits and new rites of passage for today's youth. Social networks are here to stay, so get ready to be friended.

THE SOCIAL WEB

Today's teens log a lot of screen time. Much like the teens of the 1950s and 1960s chatting on the telephone while working on homework, today's teens do the same thing—in very different ways. Instant messaging and text messaging have taken the place of hours-long after-school phone chats. They may be downloading songs and ringtones while paging through several browser windows, carrying on multiple conversations, and working on their homework all at the same time. The Internet gives teens many ways to occupy their time, and social networking has risen rapidly in popularity.

Social networking grew out of the first generation of Internet Web sites. The early emphasis of the Web was on passive consumption, much like a television show—you could read and look, but that was about it. The social Web, commonly referred to as Web 2.0, turned that model on its head. With more advanced and sophisticated programming, Internet users were presented with sites where consumption was encouraged, but contribution was also part of the mix. Early examples of this included commenting or e-mailing reactions to blog posts or news stories.

Everything changed with the addition of social networking to existing sites and with the development of sites solely devoted to user contributions. Now, users are active participants rather than passive consumers. They can instantly make comments, communicate their status, customize the way they see different pages on different sites, and create a sense of community that older people would recognize if teens were doing the same activities in a backyard or basement—socializing together, sharing and creating the new youth culture.

With social networking, teens are in control. If their time is highly scheduled, they can communicate with friends asynchronously. This gives them the opportunity to connect whenever they have downtime. Today's teens defy physical limitations on their lives through the use of social networking and online social space. The situation can be seen as a response to the changing offline culture and the ways in which the lives of young people have altered over the last 20 to 30 years.

LOSS OF PUBLIC SPACE

It has been observed that one of the most striking characteristics of today's teen population is the lack of public space available to them. Even before the "cocooning" trend observed after 9/11, when public spaces outside the home began to be regarded as unsafe and potentially threatening, teens have experienced a slow erosion of parental trust and autonomy as their lives have become increasingly full of activities that purport to "keep them busy and out of trouble," as well as activities that take place under the auspices of close adult supervision. Organized activities in the private sphere have become an integral part of the adolescent experience, rather than casual and informal activities taking place in the public sphere. Further complicating matters are the shifted body clocks of teens, who tend to experience peak alertness hours in late evening when few places outside the home are open to them. Teens in rural areas and suburbs are often also restricted by a lack of transportation—if you do not have ready access to a vehicle, then you usually cannot travel between far-flung friends' houses or to the only public destinations that might be miles away.

As a result of this loss of space, social media researcher danah boyd (2006) offers the opinion that one of the reasons teens use social networking sites is to take advantage of so-called "digital publics" in the absence of physical space once available to youth. With popular gathering places such as malls setting limits of how many young people can gather together at one time, a dearth of businesses willing to cater to teen customers, and home-based entertainment system use on the rise, it is easy to see how staying at home has become the new version of "going out." boyd asserts that "[social networking sites] substitute for the types of publics that most adults took for granted growing up, but are now inaccessible for many young people—neighborhood basketball courts, malls, parks, etc. Youth are trying to map out a public youth territory for themselves, removed from adult culture. They are doing so online because their mobility and control over physical space is heavily curtailed and monitored." Youth-serving librarians sometimes refer to this phenomenon as a lack of "third space." Third spaces are places where youth are welcomed other than school and home—another outlet in the community where they feel welcome to spend time and have some level of ownership in the space. Libraries that strive to be that third place for teens can also provide access to many teens' chosen third place—online spaces.

The struggle to find third spaces is often acutely felt by the large numbers of suburban teens in America. William Hamilton of the *New York Times* interviewed designers in 1999 about the lack of spaces being planned in suburban developments for teens, noting that the selection of adult-free spaces is considered integral to adolescent development. The experts Hamilton interviewed claimed that by incorporating this knowledge into suburban design, teenaged "anxieties" could be somewhat alleviated: Teens "need a place to congregate in and to call their own; it is a critical aspect of relieving the awkward loneliness of adolescence. Between home and school—spheres compromised by the presence of parents or the pressure of performance—places for teen-agers in the suburbs are as uncommon as sidewalks" (Hamilton, 1999).

With the rise of restrictions on physical freedom, digital publics that formed through social networking can provide an important avenue of communication, socialization, and connection for teens who are all too often kept from these identity tasks in person. Social networking, then, provides a niche online that can act as their "third space." Traditional face-to-face contact is replaced with online presence and helps with identity formation. These digital publics are areas they claim as their own for gathering, discourse, and experimentation in lieu of available physical space.

This can have unexpected benefits, given that teens today can now make powerful connections with their peers from other regions and countries that turn traditional notions of pen-pal association on their heads. Teens use social networking sites not only to virtually meet up and interact with their real-life peers, but also to build international peer groups and participate in larger global efforts that align with their formative values. Teens can find audiences that challenge them, validate their beliefs, or confront their preconceptions about the world.

THE ONLINE LIFE

By and large, teens' online lives look very similar to their offline lives. Their use of social networks to collaborate and socialize is not unlike the ways in which teens of the past used malls, parks, backyards, and basements.

According to a 2007 study from the Pew Internet and American Life Project, more than half of American teens ages 12–17 who are online use social networking sites. Over half of these teens have used sites such as MySpace or Facebook and have created a personal profile. Forty-eight percent of this population log in to their Web sites at least once per day. Girls ages 15–17 are more likely to have used the sites—70 percent in comparison with 54 percent of boys in this age range (Lenhart et al., 2007). They use the sites to stay in touch with friends—even those they see frequently. They make plans with existing friends for offline activities or reach out to other users and make new friends. Seventeen percent of teens, particularly older boys, use social networking sites to flirt. Social networking has given teens a new avenue for the age-old practice of just hanging out.

Precedents to today's social networking sites were online journals and diaries (Diaryland, Xanga, etc.) as well as Orkut, Friendster, and other more-or-less exclusive sites that demanded in-person knowledge of someone who could vouch you into the site so that you could gain traction. Among American teens, MySpace and Facebook have emerged supreme as the second generation of social networking. The most popular site is MySpace: the 2007 Pew study indicated that 85 percent of teens surveyed have a profile on this site. At the time, 7 percent of teens had a user profile on Facebook; today numbers are climbing, now that Facebook has done away with requiring membership in a participating offline educational institution. Facebook skews towards an older audience, tending to attract older teens and adults, as well as those for whom MySpace does not hold appeal.

The larger Web is social, too: social networking is not confined to sites specially designed for social networking. In fact, you would be hard pressed to find a successful Web site these days that does not make user experience social—for example, look at Amazon or YouTube. These sites successfully incorporate many social networking elements such as profiles, comments, and groups based around shared interests. Today's Web is one where the ultimate user experience includes highly social aspects—no matter the user's age. Once online, teens alter their profiles frequently through a process called "profile pimping." This can mean using backgrounds, pictures, designs, and widgets (mini-applications that can be easily added to a social networking page) on a profile to create a look that says something about the teen user. Profile pages can be unique and individualistic; the process is similar to decorating a bedroom and having a space that reflects your life. Alternately, teens can reaffirm the zeitgeist through popular applications that are used widely by other youth, such as glitter graphics or badges that proclaim their membership in a group. A variety of information is included on profiles, but first names or pseudonyms as a user name (sometimes called "handles") and photos are standard. Many include false information on their profiles both for self-protection and for fun. Users can also make their profile private, or visible only to friends. Forty-five percent of social networking teens have opted to allow only friends to see their profile. Another Pew survey showed that many teens establish a balance by confining sensitive information to a small trusted network while being active in a wider community in order to have their profile more widely viewed. Through these varying levels of profile access, they can control their personal information while still remaining active in a larger community.

Social networking sites feature a variety of messaging options, some of which are public and others which are private. Leaving comments on a MySpace page or using a friend's Wall on Facebook lets users not only contact an individual friend, but also send a message to that larger group of friends as well. For example, think about how teens love to decorate friend's lockers on birthdays or before a big athletic event. This is the same action, writ much larger and used much more frequently. You can openly make a statement about your relationships in front of an audience online—public display of affection with impact! Additionally, instead of passing notes in class you can privately message friends through social networking sites. This messaging option acts very much like e-mail, and to some extent many teens have abandoned other e-mail services in order to consolidate all messaging onto their social networking site or sites of choice. Also, some social networking sites offer embedded chat or instant messaging (IM) modules when users are online. These powerful communication tools make it possible for teens to pick an online home and connect seamlessly with other users in a multitude of ways.

In these ways, many offline habits from teen life have transferred successfully to the virtual realm. Communication is conducted both publicly and privately on social networking spaces. Privately, users can communicate directly with each other through instant messages. Although teens still use e-mail to some extent, their primary method of online communication is via IM. The more public forms of communication offer many more options such as poking, nudging, and posting a comment or kudos to the larger group.

Additionally, teens originally gravitated toward social networking sites for specific reasons. MySpace emerged in 2003 as a product of music lovers in Los Angeles. Its use was intended specifically to complement the independent music scene and to facilitate in-person socializing. MySpace members tend to use pseudonyms rather than their real names, and although the MySpace Terms of Use agreement requires members to be at least 14 years old, there are many younger members falsifying their birth dates to join. Conversely, Facebook was invented in a university setting in 2004 and concentrated on linking people to each other through academic affiliations, using their real names and locations. The network grew in 2006 by allowing anyone to join despite their enrollment in higher education, and it maintains its original goal of organizing people in relationship to real-life associations. Users of Facebook tend to be older than those on MySpace (Atal, 2007).

One prominent feature of social networking is how your offline social groups can impact your online life. For example, there is a reason young Brazilians flock to Orkut—because other young Brazilians use the service. By sticking with a service that corresponds geographically with your offline social group, you have the opportunity to reinforce offline social norms through the electronic medium.

Meeting people and finding new friends has been completely transformed with the advent of social networking. Rather than the traditional method of meeting someone in person and then going about discovering his or her interests and values, social networking allows users to search for very specific interests before making personal connections. It is easy to find new people with whom you have something in common. Teens project themselves in a virtual world and affiliate themselves with the social groups of their choice. They can share musings, videos, and photos with friends and family members who may be long-distance, or they can reinvent themselves and create new personas that they might not feel able to try on in their offline life.

Many online friendships are composed of people known by one another in the real world. However, networks may be formed by teens who discover each other creatively. A comment on one's video, photos, or writing may lead the creator to want to investigate the commentator further by clicking on his or her profile. The outcome could well be an exchange and dialogue on common interests or values.

SCHOOLWORK GOES ONLINE

Social networks also reflect the offline need to study and make sense of academic materials. Teens can ask each other for help with particular problems online or make plans to get together to study offline. The National School Boards Association issued a white paper in 2007 encouraging the use of social networking in schools to reinforce the learning communities that are growing student-to-student online—they found that over half of all students using social networks talk "specifically about homework" (National School Boards Association, 2007).

However, taking homework online has not always been a smooth process. There are problems inherent in transforming offline practices into online ones. What was once relatively invisible to schools is now quite public online. Study groups gathering in a friend's basement or a coffee shop still take place, but students are now just as likely to meet virtually to accomplish the same tasks. For example, a member group on a social networking site that grows exponentially runs the risk of appearing similar to cheating to adult authority figures who have not grown up in this digital world. That is what happened to Chris Avenir, a student at Ryerson University. He was an administrator of a Facebook study group designed to connect students attending several different sections of a chemistry class, where they collaborated to work on homework problems online. The group grew to 146 members, and Avenir was subsequently caught in controversy when he was charged with academic misconduct. Had this study group been a small offline group of friends who met to help each other in the school library or student union, their activity would have gone relatively unnoticed by the general public. But because the students connected online, and their association was publicly documented, teachers and administrators did not know how to respond to this new method of students helping students. The Ryerson school newspaper said that "the issue highlights a generation gap between students who use the Internet as an informal forum and school administrators who are trying to figure out how to deal with it" (Morrow, 2008).

DIGITAL HAVES AND HAVE-NOTS

Fast Company is a magazine devoted to business and innovation. You would not expect to find a profile of a 17-year-old in its pages, but that is what happened in September 2007. Responding to her peers' desire to reinvent themselves via their MySpace profiles, Ashley Qualls started a Web site called WhateverLife, where she offered her own graphics and page layouts free of charge to visitors. She is the perfect example of the power of access to social networking. Although her family was not wealthy, being provided home Internet access led to the discovery of a lifetime: adding advertisements to her Web site enabled her to buy a new home for her family, hire a lawyer, become emancipated, and launch her first formal business venture—all before high school graduation. Social networking has been very good to Qualls. Her ability to experiment online, to add and develop content, and eventually to retool her free layout site into a business venture has empowered her to do great things through the connective influence of MySpace.

Qualls created Whateverlife in 2004 when she was 14 years old. It was a vehicle to help her share her design work with personal friends and was an outlet for her interest in coding HTML. Whateverlife flew under the radar until Qualls learned to design MySpace page layouts and graphics. Friends and acquaintances grew the site until she was posting on a daily basis and could not keep up. In only one year, her site demanded its own server to manage the traffic. But in order to rent server space, a great deal of money was needed—so Qualls turned to Google AdSense to exploit the site's heavy traffic. The more hits her site received, the more money she would make by letting Google place ads on her pages. Qualls transformed overnight from a mere layout design queen to one with her own revenue machine (Salter, 2007).

That's the power of the digital haves versus the have-nots—Ashley had been working online since the age of nine at home, able to absorb Internet culture and to learn through experimentation. A teen who has access to the Internet only once or twice a week through a heavily filtered connection at school or another public space, such as the library, would never have been able to develop this sort of idea or carry it to its natural conclusion. Although not every teen will become a digital entrepreneur, we do not want the "have-nots" to be shut out of this cultural phenomenon. If teens are not able to navigate and participate in social networks, they are being deprived of the ability to build skills that are rapidly becoming the social norms of the 21st century.

In 2006, CBS News (Hoar, 2006) noted in an article called "The Digital Divide 2.0" that "the brave new wired world is truly unforgiving to the wired-less...There are demands on American teenagers that didn't exist decades ago. Access to and familiarity with the technology that has become the medium of global business is critical." Although interviewees attest that just providing access is not enough—that teens need more education integrated with these digital skills—access and exposure are often the crucial first step. "While schools continue to make strides in bridging the Digital Divide 2.0 ... students who have gadgets at home have advantages over students who don't. They simply have more opportunities to come up with…ways to use the technology for things as diverse as researching school projects, looking for jobs, and even gaming."

ONLINE AND OFFLINE EFFECTS

Such disenfranchisement has an impact on offline lives as well. Henry Jenkins (Doyle, n.d.) from the MIT Comparative Media Studies program points out that today's "key social and cultural experiences" are being had online and "define the emerging generation's relationship to these technologies." Jenkins asserts that *access* itself is not the issue, but access that facilitates full participation in these experiences is key. He points out that unlimited home access to the Internet "is very different from what a kid can do in a public library with ten or fifteen minutes of access at a time and with no capacity to store and upload information to the Web." Youth using public-access computers, his argument continues, are subjected to more stringent filtering than their wealthier peers, and they are not only being cut off from social experiences online but also being offered a different access to information.

The social impact of limiting teens' use of social networking sites means that in addition to a participation gap, there is also an access gap. Libraries are in a unique position to offer teens access to social networking that they may not have at home or at school. Providing this access can give disenfranchised teens a way to enter the culture where they may be otherwise locked out.

Teens are sometimes denied access to learning opportunities through social networks in settings such as libraries, but they are denied far more often in schools. If educators and librarians lack familiarity with social networking, then social networking has the potential to look like mere deviance, as in the Chris Avenir anecdote. Many adults choose not to learn about social networks or how to lever them for learning activities. A Pew report called "Listening to Student Voices on Technology" indicated that teens know that their online lives at school are being curtailed, often to their detriment. The fallout from the fear of predators and the reluctance and non-training of teachers to exploit digital technology and the power of the Internet have resulted in students becoming seriously disconnected from formal learning experiences at school, which they characterize as crippling compared to their out-of-school experiences with information. "The vast majority of students report that since not every student has access to the Internet outside of school, their teachers do not make homework assignments that require use of the Internet…Other teachers try to limit these students and the Internet access in an attempt to reduce the very real differences between the experienced users and their less tech-savvy peers" (Levin and Arafeh, 2002).

The result, of course, is not to eliminate or even reduce differences between the haves and have-nots. The effects from a lack of access are simply increased, and students from both groups are severed from authentic learning opportunities.

ONLINE SPACES (DANGEROUS PLACES?)

There are compelling and worrisome tales of the dangers of access to social networks. It is easy to understand why inexperienced teachers and librarians are frightened away from providing access: the media has created frenzy over stranger danger online, and ill-informed legislation has threatened schools' and libraries' access to the Internet because of the hysteria. A culture of fear has also grown up around social networks precisely because of the democratizing nature of the Internet. Nancy Willard, educator and authority on issues related to the safe and responsible use of the Internet, says that there is a phenomenon of "disinhibition"—people do or say things on the Internet that they might be reluctant to express in real life (2007). This can lead to positive or negative results—while it may liberate teens to share opinions and friendship with others, it also allows for the free expression of negativity as well. Online bullying is a more prevalent issue than MySpace-related abductions, but we hear about it much less often.

This culture of fear relates to other offline fears that have been present in our society for far longer. The perception that social networking is leading to youth victimization is inextricably tied to the ease with which users may participate and add content online—thereby demonizing the format of online communication. A 2007 Pew report on "Teens, Privacy, and Online Social Networks" (Lenhart and Madden, 2007) found that "while many teens post their first name and photos on their profiles, they rarely post information on public profiles they believe would help strangers actually locate them such as their full name, home phone number or cell phone number." However, around half of teens surveyed in the study believed that someone could link their information together in order to discover their true identity online, if they were determined to do so. Nearly half of the teens included the name of their school on their social networking profile, and 82 percent included only their first names, with 29 percent including a last name as well. Only 2 percent listed their cell phone number. Notably, "when teens, particularly girls, talked about protection of their privacy online, their main concern was the protection of their physical self—if a piece of information could easily lead to them being contacted in person, girls would not share it readily." Boys were more likely to post personal information than girls, reinforcing the idea that much of what we are hearing about danger on the Internet is simply an extension of existing sociocultural phenomena.

The concerns about online safety are remarkably gendered in that these concerns reflect the conventional wisdom about society in general: namely, that women and girls are weak and prime targets for victimization. Correspondingly, the major hysteria over social networking to date is the perception that teens, mainly girls, are being stalked online by pedophiles and sexual deviants. This is an issue addressed by the CyberTipline of the National Center for Missing and Exploited Children, among other nonprofit entities.

Portraying Victimization

The CyberTipline (http://tcs.cybertipline.com/videos.htm) launched a national online safety awareness campaign in which they produced ads depicting threatening older men pursuing young girls based on information the girls shared online. In three of the five television ads they aired, young Caucasian teen girls are being threatened in person by older men who have accessed their online information. The fourth is a Spanish-language ad in which a female narrator talks about meeting a guy online as her room is being processed by a crime unit and her keyboard is bagged for evidence. The final ad depicts a Caucasian teen girl chatting online with friends, featuring a voiceover by Jamie Lee Curtis warning parents that sexual predators can enter their home through the Internet. Four of the five ads play directly on the gendered fear that girls are at more risk of victimization than boys and that Caucasians are more at risk than minorities, thereby projecting an old fear onto new technology.

As a result of publicity based on similar concepts, public discourse is almost totally focused on the threat of older males cyberstalking young female tweens and teens. Males are rarely if ever depicted as targets of this type of behavior, thereby transferring many of the same gendered perceptions about teen and tween behavior that people have in the offline world—that we should worry about girls more because they are weaker, are prone to succumb to older men's advances, and are easily assaulted and/or raped. Although these fears are well-founded, knowing that women are continually and pervasively targeted as victims of violence in their homes and in our society at large, they may also serve as a self-perpetuating myth, ignoring the fact that boys and young men are also targets of unwanted attention and harassment online. Additionally, cyberstalking and harassment is depicted exclusively in a heterosexual way, ignoring possible abuses that can take place for teens who are gay, lesbian, bisexual, transgendered, or otherwise genderqueer. Race is also an issue—although teens of all races are at risk, only female Caucasian teens tend to be portrayed as victims.

Other sobering statistics are trotted out to portray social networking as a menace to youth. The 2000 report "Online Victimization" from the Crimes Against Children Research Center (Finkelhor, Mitchell, and Wolak, 2000), funded through the National Center for Missing and Exploited Children, reports that 1 in 5 teens were sexually solicited online. This statistic continues to be quoted despite its outdated nature—even after a follow-up study was conducted in 2006 (Wolak, Mitchell, and Finkelhor, 2006), and the statistic dropped to 1 in 7. The study's definition of sexual solicitation was "requests to engage in sexual activities or sexual talk or give personal sexual information that were unwanted." So although the phrase "sexual solicitation" may sound like the youth were being asked to meet for sexual purposes, it appears to be used to describe any undesirable conversation with sexual content. Unfortunately, because of the limited information disclosed in the survey results, we are not sure precisely what conversational topics were mentioned. It is worth observing that frank sex talk is common among many teenagers and that this offline practice has inevitably crossed over into the online world.

Although unwelcome sexual advances are not acceptable online or offline, it is worth looking closely at the study to see what, if any, additional information can help us understand this statistic as it applies to youth using social networks.

Behind the Numbers

One piece of information worth noting is that the 1 in 5 and 1 in 7 teens who were sexually solicited online appeared to be suffering unwanted solicitation primarily from their own peer groups as well as adjacent peer groups—43 percent of all solicitations came from people under age 18, and another 30 percent came from people ages 18–25. For example, a situation might occur where a 17-year-old is solicited online by a 20-year-old (who could have conceivably attended the same school at the same time).

Taking situations such as this into consideration, nearly three-quarters of all sexual solicitation appears to be peer-to-peer harassment instead of the stereotypical "dirty old man" aggressor pursuing the young female. In other words, it appears that real life has caught up to the online world. Of course, peer-to-peer harassment is nothing to discount, whether it occurs in school hallways or in the online world. But it is wise to keep in mind that online harassment to a great extent reflects real-life harassment. The 2006 study also noted that "the Internet is apparently being used more and more for the bullying and harassment widespread among many youth peer groups." Self-reported harassment among teens went up eight percent from 2000 to 2006.

Cyberbullying

Appropriately, recent focus has shifted, and more new slogans concern themselves with the prevention of cyberbullying. One case stood out in the news for its connection to adults—Megan Meier, a 13-year-old eighth-grader in Missouri, committed suicide in 2006 after being emotionally manipulated on MySpace by the mother of a former friend. The mother wanted to exact revenge on Megan by extracting information from her and did so by posing as a 16-year-old boy on MySpace. After befriending Megan through the sock puppet account, the mother and a coworker kept up the pretense and flirted with Megan—and then turned on her and began attacking her, first in a mild way and then finally by allegedly claiming that "the world would be a better place without [Megan]" (Associated Press, 2008).

Again, peer-to-peer and even parental harassment is not a new thing. One needs only to remember the 1991 incident involving Wanda Holloway, mother of an aspiring middle-school cheerleader, who took out a hit on the mother of a fellow cheerleader in order to make sure that her daughter would win ("Wanda Holloway," 2007). Adults can play a huge role in either preventing or exacerbating harassment in the teen years, and although these examples are admittedly two of the most extreme, they remind us that the Internet and social networks did not invent new situations to be afraid of—they are merely extensions of real-life situations that can exist with or without the use of technology. In the article "Extending the School Grounds?—Bullying Experiences in Cyberspace" from the *Journal of School Health*, it is noted that "for most youth, electronic communication entails prosocial behavior aimed at developing and sustaining friendship networks and romantic relationships. Mean behaviors may therefore be just as inevitable online as they are in other social contexts" (Juvonen and Gross, 2008). They go on to indicate that youth who are "repeatedly targeted at school" have seven times greater risk of also being bullied online, and an overall 85 percent overlap between online and in-school bullying experiences. It seems that online environments are highly reflective of the real-life environments that youth live in every day, with very similar cautions and considerations (Juvonen and Gross).

Stranger Danger Goes Online

However, many adults still fear that stranger danger is made more real by the use of social networks. The popular NBC show *Dateline NBC: To Catch a Predator,* with host Chris Hansen, illustrates both the fears and the stereotypes of a nation that has failed to keep pace with its children's online escapades, naïve adults who imagine cyberspace to be the embodiment of all the real-world fears and stereotypes that have flourished in the United States for generations. The typical predator scenario involves staff members engaging in online contact with potential predators by posing as underage teens and tweens looking for sexual encounters.

The show's premise is routine and formulaic: Make contact with a potential predator online and lure the predator to a house to meet the fictional chatting youth. And then the potential predator is confronted by Hansen, who further titillates the audience by conducting a conversation with the would-be predator, including rereading graphic excerpts from a paper transcript of the illicit chats. Predators on the show are exclusively male (Go, 2007). The gendered message of fear is clear: parents should worry excessively about these crazy men who will, given any provocation, run over to their house and attack their child (most commonly depicted as female) because all men using the Internet and social networks are slavering pedophiles who have absolutely no self-control.

The *Dateline NBC* fantasy, then, is that this preconception also holds true in the online world. It attempts to convince parents that they should adopt a stance of constant vigilance and become alarmist over every interaction that their teens have on the Internet because a predator could be anywhere, ready to penetrate their homes and commit assault. Yet, the Internet is not the only way potential predators can learn about teens. Many families routinely advertise their children's names, interests, and ages in public. Although they would never dream of allowing their kids to do the same online, parents still plaster their cars with white die-cut decals advertising their kids' names and jersey numbers or their after-school activity or competitive sports league. In some communities, yard signs are also common—public acknowledgments of youth joining an activity or a team, usually featuring their names. Until adults adopt a more consistent approach to disclosing personal information in public (both online and offline), teens may discount our advice on these issues.

Social networks can also lead teens to disclose information that can later affect them in other ways. Today's teens grow up with a lot of pressure—personal digital media recorders and cell phone cameras mean that any action of theirs could be potentially passed around through social networks in an instant. Any lapse in judgment could be recorded and preserved indefinitely on the Internet, where it is much harder to eliminate all copies of a picture or video than it is in real life. They may create profiles that make sense to their peers but that reflect negatively on them when viewed through a potential employer's or college admission counselor's eyes. Teens aging into the workforce find themselves defending their profiles and social networking content as they struggle with the weakening boundaries between online and offline life.

Schools and libraries have a unique opportunity to help teens deal with the pressures that the online world causes. If we experiment with social networks and learn about the ways in which they can be used, then we are much more informed when potential issues arise, in both online and offline spaces. It makes sense to explore the worlds that teens are able to create online, to learn more about their online lives and how they intersect with their experience in offline situations. Social networking has tremendous power to be leveraged for more than merely social purposes; social networking can make learning social too.

Educator, author, and edublogger Will Richardson (2006) reminds us that the power of Web 2.0 and social networking will affect the lives of our youth in ways that we have yet to imagine; educators are especially affected by these changes. How will curriculum adapt to "students'...ability to reach audiences far beyond...classroom walls" and as it "becomes easier to bring primary sources to...students?" The very notion of literacy may change now that educators "must prepare...students to become not only readers and writers, but [also] editors and collaborators."

Although Richardson is speaking directly to educators, librarians who serve youth would do well to heed his words. Not only are students socializing in a world where they have the power to make connections and friendships far beyond any physical boundaries; they are also engaging in a new way of learning and knowing online. They are creators of content rather than mere consumers. Our libraries and learning spaces must begin to reflect the fact that 21st-century teens need access, guidance, and support using social networks.

ADVOCATING FOR YOUTH USING SOCIAL NETWORKS

It is important to remember that not all teens are using social networks, and certainly not all teens are tech-savvy. When researchers and social scientists talk about the digital divide, they are describing a very real phenomenon that is limiting the potential for today's young people to develop the skills they need to succeed in an increasingly connected world. Teens with limited access to technology and who do not have the freedom to explore the Web without overly restrictive content filtering do not have the same experiences on social networks that their more liberally connected peers have. Librarians must advocate for teen access to social networks in our schools and libraries so that all teens have access to them. In the same vein, we need to advocate our libraries' active participation in these networks so that there are valuable, information-rich resources waiting for teens to use. By making ourselves compatible with their preferred online spaces, libraries can reach teens and encourage non-users to harness the technology not just for social purposes, but also for informational and educational purposes that are amplified by the social aspect of networking sites.

Rosemary Honnold (2007) opines in *Get Connected: Tech Programs for Teens*,

> Teens often have little guidance in how to use technology. Many ignore owners' manuals in favor of "clicking to see what happens." Their sense of adventure challenges librarians to keep up with what students are doing and guide them towards safe and responsible use. As new technologies expand the scope of information literacy, teaching teens to evaluate information is more critical than ever.

We should also be aware that teens are not always using technology in the most efficient manner and may not be aware of all the resources they can use online. Even tools that may interest them and that they may take advantage of could pass under their radar. For example, Twitter is a social networking and microblogging application that many users have adopted as a complement to their online social networking personas. There is not a critical mass of teenagers yet participating on this site, but many might opt to try it if they knew that its benefits can go beyond interpersonal socialization. Instead of contacting people they know, they can subscribe to news outlets such as the *New York Times*, PBS, the BBC, and others who will then send headlines and links directly to their cell phones or Web Twitter accounts while, say, they are working on a current events report. When librarians know of and use these social networking tools, we can work to make teens aware of their advantages and potential informational value (Slatalla, 2008).

Advocacy for free access is necessary if we wish to serve teens meaningfully in libraries. Intellectual freedom and equity are paramount to teens who need to log time online in order to compete competently in this brave new online world. Just as adults are using social networking to develop and cement professional relationships, teens who join a future version of Richard Florida's (2002) "creative class" will find it absolutely imperative to develop the appropriate online skills so that they can function effectively as information age professionals. There is the potential for social networking benefits to be denied to the teens who need them the most— those who depend on their libraries to provide access because they have none or limited time online at home. This also has repercussions because online behaviors are largely not being taught in schools. Many educators also lack access to the social networking and Web tools needed to guide students in the formation of these new skills and are subjected to the same strict filtering as students. More importantly, many librarians and teachers are not participants themselves in social networks, thereby severely reducing the possibility of connecting traditional pedagogy with these next-generation tools to enhance understanding. Some adults see social networking as an immature activity or as too complex to master easily, or they have no curiosity about how social networking functions in the lives of today's youth. As librarians, we do not have this choice—we must make this social phenomenon part of our professional practice so that we can assist our patrons in 21st-century ways of connecting and knowing.

DEVELOPING SOCIAL NETWORKING SERVICES

With the swift evolution of social networking and online life, it is tempting for libraries to step back and wait for the right time to jump in. This would not be wise. Just as teen culture changes almost constantly, the new world of social networking does as well. The right time is always now, and libraries should jump in. Worry less about your library's online presence being "perfect," and worry more about simply being present in the space of "nearly now" that teens occupy online (Consortium for School Networking, 2008).

Rosemary Honnold (2007) points out that libraries have an opportunity to introduce themselves to users in a different way through social networking. "In cases where technology is perceived and used mainly for entertainment, librarians can, through resources and learning activities, help teens become lifelong learners and productive citizens." Because teens often use social networks for convenience and to keep up with their friends while on the go, this means that social networking is rapidly moving to mobile services. A library's social networking presence, then, can expand beyond even its network and stretch to reach teens wherever they happen to be as they are increasingly able to access library resources through mobile applications on cell phones and handheld devices (Fox, 2008).

Making library services and resources relevant to today's teens means aggressive repackaging of content. Too often libraries design their Web sites as paper versions of their brick and mortar services and ignore the opportunities to recreate the library in a way that is of the best use to the online user. Instead of having a "teen page" on your library Web site, consider maintaining several presences on social networking sites instead. By creating profiles on Facebook, MySpace, Bebo, or other networks, you are able to reach users on their own turf—not forcing them to leave their space to come to your library site.

Ideally, you should be able to ask vendors for assistance in customizing content widgets that can be added to different social networking platforms. Just as they are able to add games and decorations to those spaces, teens should also be able to integrate connections to their library. Many database providers, such as EBSCO and others, are able to provide code for you to use in creating widgets on your library's Web page—ask them to start developing applications that are compatible with social networking Web sites, too.

Prepare to reach teens where they are, and go cross-platform to cater to their differing demographics. Not all teens are on the hot site of the moment, nor will they be a month or a year from now. Staying light and flexible allows libraries to nimbly navigate the world of social networking.

Just as in the past we pursued consortia to purchase databases and automated catalogs, we should now collectively assist one another in reaching teens through social networking. Each community may need a particular library "brand" to reach their particular group of teens, but not all librarians are able to devote resources to the development of social networking services that complement teens' online experiences. It takes time and dedication to grow a presence on a social networking site and takes specific skills to use APIs (application programming interfaces) and build cross-platform widgets. Library systems and consortia should seriously consider pooling their resources to purchase the time of a programmer who can develop applications and widgets that bridge the gap between traditional library Web pages and social networking sites. These could include customizable options so that libraries could tailor the product to their particular teens' taste and preferences.

Frequently, 21st-century libraries strive to create the sort of lost, lamented networks described in Robert Putnam's *Bowling Alone: The Collapse and Revival of American Community* (2000). In many ways, social networks are springing up as the next generation of bowling leagues and social clubs. Instead of trying to create community from scratch, begin to recognize community in all its new forms, and seek to add value as only libraries can—especially for your teen users, who are used to seeing these networks solely as social outlets and not as the powerful tools of connection they can be when linked with gateways to the world of information. Today's librarians have a great opportunity to advocate for the use of and access to social networks for teens and to work toward developing tools and information for these sites so that libraries truly cross boundaries. Let's strive to provide access to information wherever young people connect, whether in physical library buildings or online in social networks.

WORKS CITED

Associated Press. 2008. "Mom indicted in deadly MySpace hoax." *CNN*, May 15. http://www.cnn.com/2008/CRIME/05/15/internet.suicide/index.html (accessed May 22, 2009).

Atal, Maha. 2007. "MySpace, Facebook: A tale of two cultures." *BusinessWeek*, July 2. http://www.businessweek.com/innovate/content/jul2007/id2007 072_502208.htm (accessed May 22, 2009).

boyd, danah. 2006. *Identity Production in a Networked Culture: Why Youth Heart MySpace.* http://danah.org/papers/AAAS2006.html (accessed May 22, 2009).

Consortium for School Networking. 2008. *Changing to Learn, Learning to Change.* http://www.cosn.org/ (accessed May 22, 2009.

Doyle, Robert P. N.d. "The current legislative challenge: DOPA and the participation gap." *Illinois Library Association.* http://www.ila.org/advocacy/pdf/DOPA.pdf (accessed May 22, 2009).

Finkelhor, David, Kimberly J. Mitchell, and Janis Wolak. 2000. "Online victimization: A report on the nation's youth." *Crimes Against Children Research Cen-*

ter, June. http://www.unh.edu/ccrc/pdf/jvq/CV38.pdf (accessed May 22, 2009).

Florida, Richard. 2002. *The Rise of the Creative Class.* New York: Basic Books.

Fox, Megan. 2008. "Trends in mobile tools & applications for libraries." *Megan's Links for Librarians and Library Students,* June 19. http://web.simmons.edu/~fox/pda/il2_07_fox.pdf (accessed May 22, 2009).

Go, Jesamyn. 2007. "Where are the female predators?" *Inside Dateline,* February 20. http://insidedateline.msnbc.msn.com/archive/category/1035.aspx?p=2 (accessed May 22, 2009).

Hamilton, William. 1999. "How suburban design is failing teen-agers." *New York Times,* May 6. http://tinyurl.com/op9p7u (accessed May 22, 2009).

Hoar, Jennifer. 2006. "The digital divide 2.0." CBS News, June 15. http://www.cbsnews.com/stories/2006/06/09/gentech/main1699023.shtml (accessed May 22, 2009).

Honnold, Rosemary. 2007. *Get Connected: Tech Programs for Teens.* New York: Neal-Schumann Publishers.

Juvonen, Jaana, and Elisheva Gross. 2008. "Extending the school grounds?—Bullying experiences in cyberspace." *Journal of School Health* 78 (9): 496–505.

Lenhart, Amanda, and Mary Madden. 2007. *Teens, Privacy and Online Social Networks: How Teens Manage Their Online Identities and Personal Information in the Age of MySpace.* Pew Internet, April 18. http://www.pewinternet.org/PPF/r/211/report_display.asp (accessed May 22, 2009).

Lenhart, Amanda, Mary Madden, Alexandra Rankin, and Aarong Smith. 2007. *Teens and Social Media.* Pew Internet. http://www.pewinternet.org/PPF/r/230/report_display.asp (accessed May 22, 2009).

Levin, Douglas, and Sousan Arafeh. 2002. *The Digital Disconnect: The Widening Gap between internet-Savvy Students and Their Schools.* Pew Internet. http://www.pewinternet.org/PPF/r/67/report_display.asp (accessed May 22, 2009).

Morrow, Adrian. 2008. "School moves to police students online." *The Eyeopener,* March 5. http://www.theeyeopener.com/article/3816 (accessed May 22, 2009).

National School Boards Association. 2007. "Creating & connecting//Research and guidelines on online social—and educational—networking." *National School Boards Association,* July. http://www.nsba.org/SecondaryMenu/TLN/CreatingandConnecting.aspx (accessed May 22, 2009).

Putnam, Robert D. 2000. *Bowling Alone: The Collapse and Revival of American Community.* New York: Simon & Schuster.

Richardson, Will. 2006. *Blogs, Wikis, Podcasts, and Other Powerful Web Tools for Classrooms.* Thousand Oaks, CA: Corwin Press.

Salter, Chuck. 2007. "Girl power." *Fast Company,* September. http://www.fastcompany.com/magazine/118/girl-power.html (accessed May 22, 2009).

Slatalla, Michelle. 2008. "If you can't let go, Twitter." *New York Times,* February 14. http://tinyurl.com/p5fjdb (accessed May 22, 2009).

"Wanda Holloway." *Almanac of Famous People,* 9th ed. Thomson Gale, 2007. Reproduced in *Biography Resource Center.* Farmington Hills, MI: Gale, 2009. http://0-galenet.galegroup.com.sable.jefferson.lib.co.us/servlet/BioRC (accessed May 22, 2009).

Willard, Nancy. 2007. *Cyber-Safe Kids, Cyber-Savvy Teens: Helping Young People Learn to Use the Internet Safely and Responsibly.* San Francisco: Jossey-Bass.

Wolak, Janis, Kimberly Mitchell, and David Finkelhor. 2006. "Online victimization of youth: Five years later." *National Center for Missing & Exploited Children.* http://www.missingkids.com/en_US/publications/NC167.pdf (accessed May 22, 2009).

3

◇ ◇ ◇

TECHNOLOGY IN THE CLASSROOM: AN EDUCATOR'S PERSPECTIVE

Michelle Pearson

21ST-CENTURY SKILLS

In an era of education where standards-based learning is tied to the larger concept of 21st-century skills, it is critical for educators, librarians, and professionals working in the larger community to realize that interactive technology is here to stay. Students in the middle levels and above often choose to access information using media or technology, rather than employing what would have been more traditional methods in the classroom (Malone, 2008). Through the use of basic technologies such as PowerPoint, Word, and podcasting, students share what they learn through the hardware they use daily—their computer and their iPod. More and more, they also access and use advanced media tools from the Internet that enhance how they learn, share, and interact with others. Facebook, MySpace, iSlide, wikis, blogs, Twitter, and Google Earth play a distinct role in the lives of students that teachers are now encountering in the classroom.

Educators and librarians are rapidly starting to realize that in order to engage students in learning, technology tools need to be used effectively to encourage higher-level thinking skills and the application of analysis and critical thinking to the content being studied, while at the same time instructing them in the ethical use of resources. The various technologies integrated into the classroom are based on the needs and desires of the students, as well as how these applications fit the desired outcomes.

Wikis have impacted tech-savvy schools in full force. With the creation of wikispaces.com and pbwiki.com, teachers and students now create their own resources to reflect what they are learning in the classroom. For basic uses such as a classroom homework site to a more developed page that serves as a student's online work portfolio, wikis come in all shapes and sizes and are being used in a multitude of ways by students and educators. An overview of dynamic use of this technology by Hulstrom Options K–8 School in Colorado's Adams County may be found at http://hulstromhomework.pbwiki.com.

By choice, Hulstrom Options students generally access an online version of a document before referencing something in print. This is demonstrated by the high use of the online homework reference system at school and the use of personal wikis by students as research and writing portfolios. For example, with over 10,000 hits per month, the Hulstrom homework wiki has quickly taken the place of the traditional student planner. When surveyed, 92 percent of students at the school said that they would prefer to access information on a wiki rather than through a print source such as their planner (Pearson, 2008).

A complete transition to electronic resources may not be possible at this time as a result of many factors, including lack of personal computers in the homes of students, limited Internet access at home and at school, and limited skills in creating wikis for personal use. However, librarians and technology staff at Hulstrom Options play a key role in ensuring that students gain adequate access to the Internet and cultivate the skills in using it, so that they can obtain information and complete required projects and research housed on student wikis.

Personal social networking affects students inside and outside the classroom. The skills students are using to create and manage their own social networking sites easily transfer to educational presentations and assessments. As the generation of students between the ages of 8 and 16 continually gain more access to technology, their skill set is changing on a continual basis and is reflected in the quality and differentiation shown in projects turned in for a grade.

For example, a case study could be students at Hulstrom Options who have been working with several local nonprofits to develop programs and materials about local history for the community. When posed with the question of "What brochure, flier, or Web page would you like to create to interpret the history of local sites for a large regional collaborative project?"—their answer was simple: "none." Rather, they elected to brainstorm ideas for projects based on their uses of technology. The result over the last three years has been a host of podcasts, blogs, and Twitters, all of which have been solely created by the students yet guided by standards and larger educational and preservation goals selected by the educator, school, and district. Classroom time has been spent on editing, discussion of subject matter, development of content, and the brainstorming of ideas to post on any of these virtual venues. The majority of the students, whether they own or use a mobile device or not, are adept at using a variety of social networking sites because of how they use them to communicate with their peer group. Transferring these personal technology skills used to communicate with friends from the home environment to the school environment is almost seamless. Students tend to select more creative assignments to turn in, or pose alternative self-directed assessments to the educator for approval, because of the larger repertoire of skills, technology content, and Web sites they are using outside of the classroom.

As students have become increasingly more skilled and technologically savvy in the classroom, they often are more aware of applications, downloads, widgets, and modules available for certain software applications because they use them on their own personal sites. Take the examples of Slide (http://www.slide.com) and Flickr (http://www.flickr.com). Many educators do not know how to use these applications within the context of the classroom, but students regularly embed them in portions of their wiki, PowerPoint, and video podcasting projects because they have "experience tinkering with them on their own time" (Fentum, 2008). As an example, in the last five years, the shift from traditional research-based personal endeavors required in the International Baccalaureate program (IB) has moved toward media-based projects by a tenfold. According to a local judge in Colorado's Adams 12 school district, students are presenting their learning with the use of the tools of their generation: Mac-edited movies, cell phone video technology, blogs, and higher technology-based presentations are now the normal end result rather than other types of traditional presentations such as research papers, PowerPoint presentations, or photo montages. A judge may still see the photo montage, but it will be in the form of a slide show using iSlide, a popular widget used by students on social networking sites.

Additionally, students have become more adept at developing core keyword searches for topics of interest because they regularly search many different social networking sites. Hulstrom Options has found it particularly useful to start a discussion with students about keyword searching by placing the lesson in the context of how they search for items and people on their own time. And searching almost always takes them to maps, mapping software, geo-caching, and Google Earth.

Assistant professor Christopher Jennings has worked extensively with the application of Google Earth in the classroom and has seen the impact it can have on students through interactive instruction. He states, "Google Earth is now being used in conjunction with primary sources in the classroom to enhance instruction and provide an additional visual medium for students and teachers to access" (2005). For example, a primary source map can be imported into Google Earth as an overlay image at the exact location represented in the map General Washington created and used to help defeat the British Troops from December 26, 1776, to January 3, 1777. Students can view the map and compare it to what the location looks like today by changing its transparency and zooming into the location. In addition, students can make certain map features such as borders, roads, county lines, cities, and other markers visible. By combining these features, students gain a new understanding and level of learning: what took place, the accuracy of the map, the lines General Washington drew for troops to march that are now roadways, and other factors that cannot be comprehended without combining a primary source with this type of technology. From a social networking perspective, students and teachers collaborate in Google Earth Community (http://bbs.keyhole.com/ubb/ubbthreads.php/Cat/0), posting their files, welcoming comments on then, and discovering new ways to use Google Earth as a learning tool.

Students access Google Earth on their own time and in their own way but have rarely used it in the classroom for practical applications tied to science, social studies, and math. Now Google Earth and geo-caching are being used by educators to provide an interactive medium and "live data" for students to reference. Although mapping software still has some drawbacks (such as when the satellite images are a year or two old), they provide more current data than a textbook in the classroom setting. As one student put it, "Google Earth and caching using satellite points are valid real-life skills that we will use. I won't be carrying a textbook around when I graduate college, but I will most likely have my GPS" (Pearson, 2008).

Educators need to clearly understand, and be able to apply to their classroom, 21st-century learning skills in order to reach this next generation of students. This is becoming more of a dividing force in the school environment. For the last 20 or so years, the educational community has been able to integrate the use of technology in the classroom at a somewhat slower pace than what they are being asked to do currently. Because students are asking, and quite frankly demanding, to use the skills they are familiar with, teachers have to learn about and use many of these social networks themselves so that they understand how they can be used in an educational context. Teachers who have never dreamed of using Facebook, Twitter, Ping, MySpace, LinkedIn, and other sites are now joining in the social networking community so that they can understand and "keep up with" their students. In this way, when a student approaches and asks to blog or Twitter on a topic, rather than keeping a traditional journal, the teacher can decide what would be appropriate for the assessment.

TEACHER AND LIBRARIAN CONNECTIONS

Making real-life connections is essential to teaching students. It can be very effective in reaching at-risk populations and second-language students as well, given that much of their free time is spent on the Internet if they have access to a computer or PDA. Students want access to information and are fast becoming masters at categorizing the media they interact with on a daily basis. If educators are preparing students for jobs that may not even exist yet, then it is critical that we teach them transferable skills and strategies that they can apply to their own personal learning, to their interactions in the community, and to the workplace. This is where it is truly important to have the collaboration and support of an experienced librarian as a partner in educating your students. Most teachers do not have all of the content knowledge or skills-based knowledge in new technologies to fully teach these tools to students and instruct in the classrooms on a daily basis. Libraries need to be a resource place for learning in print and digitally, and we as educators need to truly focus on allowing partnerships to be fostered between librarians and content specialists so that multilevel learning can take place in a classroom for students.

Many students are directed to computers available at the public library, whose staff and budgeting teams are feeling the impact of this increased need for access to the Internet. For instance, the Mamie Doud Eisenhower Public Library in Broomfield, Colorado, has seen a 21.7 percent overall increase in the use of computers for online access over the last three years. Most of the frontline staff at any local public library note a high patron demand for Internet availability at their location (Depp, 2008).

Some of the most successful programming that takes place in the Mamie Doud Eisenhower Public Library comes from the highly skilled teen staff and youth teen advisory board (TAB) group at the library. Directed by the

TAB, the librarians provide a wealth of classes that support what students want and need when they are using their library and at the same time being a teen! From programs such as "Creating Your Own Podcast" to "Nanotechnology," the librarians are on the edge, leading social networking technologies that engage students in their free time as well as supporting the learning that students of this generation want. With sections on their Web site aptly titled "Your Life, Your Voice" and the newsletter "411," they bridge the gap between learning in a contained environment, such as a classroom, and learning at your public library (http://www.broomfield.org/library/teenzone/TZ_Homepage.shtml). Again, this rock-solid format gives real-life connections to students while developing the skills and interests that make learning more interactive in the classroom. Wouldn't it be amazing to further develop this collaboration between the public school and the public library through directed programming that fosters creativity with the use of technology?

Howard Rheingold, author of the 2002 book *Smart Mobs*, frequently writes about the up-and-coming digital society. On his Web site he states, "Increasingly, technology furnishes the tools we can use to help make our cities and our planet work in a more humane and sustainable manner. But whether these tools can build better tomorrows is up to the people who use them" (Rheingold 1998). Almost any educator or student can confirm Rheingold's statement, but the question continues to be, exactly when and how do we teach students this concept? With the increased focus on standardized testing in the classroom, it is more important than ever to look at how to effectively integrate multiple styles of learning, technology, and content into an educational package that addresses a diverse classroom, a collage of learning styles, and a focused set of desired outcomes. This can be accomplished only through collaboration with the librarian. Teachers can no longer instruct alone in an isolated world; the partnership between a librarian and an educator makes the true difference in what and how our students learn and how they will become productive citizens in a digitally driven future society.

WORKS CITED

Depp, Roberta. 2008. *Mamie Doud Eisenhower Public Library Director's Report.* Broomfield, CO: City of Broomfield, Broomfield Library Foundation.
Fentum, Lexie. 2008. Interview by Michelle Pearson, May 20.
Jennings, Christopher. 2005. "Teaching with primary sources and Google Earth." Instructional class at the Metropolitan State College of Denver. Denver, CO.

Malone, Jason. 2008. "Building bridges: Technology in the classroom." Talk presented at the Building Bridges Conference, September. Fort Collins, CO.

Pearson, Michelle. 2008. "Survey of Hulstrom Options students on their technology preferences." May–June. Northglenn, CO.

Rheingold, Howard. 1998. *Maps + Databases + Internet = New Scientific, Civic, and Political Tools.* http://www.rheingold.com/texts/internet/gis.html (accessed May 22, 2009).

4

$$\diamond \; \diamond \; \diamond$$

PRACTICAL APPLICATIONS: LIBRARIES ONLINE

Jenna Obee

SOCIAL NETWORKING SITES

In February 2008, MySpace generated 65.7 million visitors a month within the United States, with nearly a billion hits per month total (Freiert, 2008). In comparison, Facebook had 28.5 million visitors.

By mid-2008, Facebook surpassed MySpace and became the largest worldwide social network. In the United States alone, MySpace still had 76 million unique visitors, while Facebook had 54.5 million unique visitors. However, Facebook's growth rate in the United States averaged 3.8 percent between mid-2007 and mid-2008 compared to 0.8 percent for MySpace during the same time span (Arrington, 2009). This illustrates the rapid growth of social networking and how quickly things change—even as you read this book. The latest statistics can be found at comScore, using the keywords "Social Networking" at http://www.comscore.com/Press_Events/Press_Releases. Many teens maintain profiles on both sites.

This chapter examines popular social networking options that may be useful for a library wishing to reach their teen patrons, including examples of how other libraries are already using these popular services.

The Big Players

Facebook

Facebook (http://www.facebook.com) draws in users with applications. Anyone can design an application and profit from the advertising (*Economist*, 2007). There are applications to infect your friends with zombie bites, share bumper stickers, send hugs, and much more. For instance, there is an application called "flair" in which you choose graphics to give to your friends. The graphics look like buttons, and anyone can make a new one by uploading a photo. When you send flair to your friends, you get points that allow you to purchase your own flair. Anyone with the flair application installed on her Facebook page has a bulletin board to post her flair for others to see. There are also popular applications that involve alcohol and sex. That is why so few libraries add applications to their Facebook page, despite frequent requests to do so.

The other major activity on Facebook is becoming a fan of your favorite celebrity or show. Being a fan allows the user to get updates via bulletins and to participate in fun activities such as quizzes on a topic. One of the most popular fansites is the Twilight page, founded in January 2008. As of May 2009, it had attracted 2,360,800 fans.

Facebook has a comments section they call FunSpace. You can set the page privacy to moderate comments received. Popularity on Facebook is determined by the number of friends you have, the comments on your FunSpace, and how much your applications are used. Most teens will add any application or friend.

Facebook allows institutions to create pages as well. When a user joins a group, it shows up on his navigation screen. Allowing a patron to join your library group will put a link to the library's Facebook page on that user's profile. Search for "public library" in the groups category to find examples. For example, the Poughkeepsie (NY) Public Library District (http://www.facebook.com/pages/Teen-Page/39343566877) has a Facebook group for its teen patrons. They post program and summer reading details and photos of teens in the library and allow members of their group to participate in a book-related forum and post on their FunSpace. It also has links to the library Web page.

Nonprofit organizations can also create a Facebook page. Users can "become a fan" of the page, which gives them a link to the organization's Facebook page on their profile. The Young Adult Library Services Association's (YALSA) Facebook page (http://www.facebook.com/pages/YALSA/35222707784?ref=s) has links to the ALA Web site, information about the group, photos, a forum for discussion, and an area for comments on its FunSpace. Other organizations with groups of interest to teens include the Society of Young Publishers and Friends (http://www.thesyp.org.uk) as well as Room To Read's (http://www.roomtoread.org) "I donated my books to support global literacy" group.

MySpace

The mammoth beast of the social networking world, MySpace (http://www.myspace.com) also seems to be a favorite of teens based on word of mouth.

Social status within the site is determined by numbers of friends and comments. Teens have publicly visible conversations via comments, rather than in private where no one can see that they are talking to lots of people. It is very common for teens to leave random messages (e.g., "sup?") on their friends' comment spaces, just to get their own face out on other pages. You can set comments to be approved by you before they are posted on MySpace.

Because having a high friend number is a sign of social success, teens will "friend" just about anyone. People who show up as top friends are most important to them. Teens will want to friend your library MySpace page, if only to have one more friend in their count. Because teens look at their friends' lists of friends to find new friends, you will also gain interest by being seen. Encourage your regular patrons to move the library's MySpace page to their top friends; however, be cautious of showing favoritism by putting specific teens in your library's top friends list.

Many libraries have MySpace pages to advertise library services. Hennepin County (MN) Library's MySpace page (http://www.myspace.com/hennepincountylibrary) links to library services, including a catalog search box, online reviews, and a blog of library activities. The Wendt Library at University of Wisconsin–Madison (http://www.myspace.com/wendt_library) has put their library blog onto their MySpace page with a widget. They also include a list of all the other ways to contact them online, including instant messaging and other social networking sites.

It is possible to customize your MySpace page to appear similar to your teen Web site. An example is Denver (CO) Public Library's Teen MySpace page (http://www.myspace.com/denver_evolver), where library staff have created a background and color scheme that is very similar to their Web site (http://teens.denverlibrary.org). Links to reviews and news take you directly to their site, so the information is not duplicated. MySpace provides a profile editor from which you can upload backgrounds and choose colors, fonts, and layout.

Some teen advisory boards have MySpace pages where they share what the group is doing, including minutes from their meetings. Often members are the friends highlighted in the top friends space. Information regarding meeting times, activities, and how to join is highlighted. Rolling Hills (MO) Consolidated Library's Teen Advisory Group (http://www.myspace.com/rhclteens) features a calendar of events that only their members can access.

Many authors create MySpace pages to advertise their books and give fans a place to meet them. Authors post comments about upcoming publications or local visits on the library's MySpace page. Also, some authors may request to be added to a library site's friends list, giving both the author and the library some extra advertising.

MySpace also hosts groups, where a number of users can create a community with a profile based on a certain subject. Users can join the group to participate in posting bulletins or in discussions in the group's forum. For instance, libraries have formed a group called "Libraries on MySpace" (http://groups.myspace.com/myspacelibraries) to connect with other library profiles. Teens have formed groups to discuss their personal interests. Since its launch in July 2004, the official MySpace Music fansite of the Jonas Brothers had generated 2,111,132 comments.

myYearbook

Used primarily by high school students myYearbook (http://www.myyearbook.com) is very similar to MySpace. The major difference is that on myYearbook, everything you do either earns or costs Lunch Money, or L$. myYearbook highlights online safety messages and gives L$ for completing safety surveys. It also features teen writing on the myMag page. Users can post personal writing, covering topics from suicide and self-mutilation to free speech to commercial reviews. Readers then have the opportunity to comment on the articles, opening dialogue between members.

It is also possible to create groups on myYearbook. Users can join a group, but it does not show up on their main page. Although a search of current groups brings up nothing library-related, it may be possible to start a library page and get teens to join.

LiveJournal

LiveJournal (http://www.livejournal.com)—commonly called LJ—is a combination of social networking and blogging communities. Its primary purpose is to host blogs, which are put there by users. It also provides friends lists and the capability to comment, so a users' friends can interact with blogs he or she has posted. Becoming friends with a user allows you to see his blog posts on your main page. Also, other friends can see your friends' posts, and they use that to create new connections.

LJ provides statistics on their users on a page that is updated daily (http://www.livejournal.com/stats.bml). It shows clearly that the vast majority of users are female Americans from 18 to 21 years old. Although this age range is slightly higher than that of the public library's usual teen population, it will be interesting to see if the younger crowd starts using LJ as they age, and if current users will stick with it into the future.

This would be a useful tool for libraries, once they have marketed and convinced patrons to use it. The library could publish blogs on current happenings and allow users to friend their page, putting the library on the patron's screen every day.

Twitter

Twitter (http://www.twitter.com), a Web site that enables quick and constant communication between teens (as well as Oprah, Ashton Kutcher, Michael Phelps, Britney Spears, Dave Matthews, and Eli Manning), is exploding. As of April 2009, its United States users jumped to 17 million, a 3,000 percent gain from the previous year (Lipsman, 2009). Twitter takes a single feature of most social networking sites—status updates called "tweets"—and makes it a primary source. Status updates allow the user to post short messages—usually what they are currently doing—that can then be read by other users. Many users keep their Twitter link available at all times so that they can see whatever is coming in, including having tweets sent to their mobile devices. Users "follow" others, receiving tweets on their main page. You do not have to register with Twitter to view the tweets a user sends out.

Teens use Twitter primarily to discuss the mundane. Users give updates on their day, send out links to interesting articles, or ask questions of their colleagues and friends. Twitter allows a user to reply directly to another user—but the reply is posted to everyone following that user. However, that does not mean Twitter communication is always inconsequential. It has been used in more extreme situations as well. Twitter publicized the story of an American journalist who was freed from an Egyptian jail in just a few hours thanks to his colleagues' response when he sent out the tweet "arrested" (Simon, 2008).

Many organizations use Twitter to advertise ongoing activities or changes to their Web site. Libraries use Twitter to send out notices of events or news. Patrons "follow" the library and receive the notices immediately. Douglas County Libraries in Colorado has a Twitter following at http://twitter.com/DCLcolorado. A word of warning—do not overwhelm Twitter fans. Users that publish upwards of 3–4 tweets in a day are often considered annoying. One per day is plenty.

Ning

Ning (http://www.ning.com) allows users to create their own social networking sites based on a specific interest. Users create a profile for themselves and may then join networks. Anyone can create a network of their own.

Kirkland (WA) Library has a teen Ning (http://kirklandlibraryteen. ning.com) that is meant primarily to discuss books but that also includes news about the library and events. Roselle (IL) Public Library District (http://rosellelibrary.ning.com/) created a network for staff, patrons, and supporters. They post library news and events, new titles, photos, and videos and ask members to contribute to the forums. They also have a catalog search and allow library card holders to log in to their account from the Ning page.

There is also a Ning for young adult librarians looking to use Web 2.0 applications in their libraries, called "Library Youth and Teen Services 2.0" (http://libraryyouth.ning.com). Members use the forums to discuss projects they are working on and look for examples and input from other librarians.

Another popular Ning among libraries is Nerdfighters, the network created by Printz award–winning author John Green and his brother Hank Green (http://nerdfighters.ning.com/). John and Hank post vlogs (video blogs) about their day-to-day lives, and other members are encouraged to post as well. They host a forum, put up polls, collect photos, and generally market books and all things "nerdy." With over 23,500 members, this is one of the largest specialized social networking sites available.

Other Popular Social Networking Options

Some social networking sites cater to niche markets. BlackPlanet.com and UrbanChat.com, for African Americans, focus on cultural interests such as music, fashion, sports, and business. AsianTown.NET is a very similar option for Asian Americans. CafeMom caters to mothers. These sites are growing in popularity as people try to find personalized communities. They do not appear to be used by libraries, nor is there an obvious way to do so.

The United States is not the only country with a growing social networking interest. Most hi5 users are Latin American, but primary users tend to be Spanish speakers, so it does have some interest in the United States. Orkut is popular in Brazil and India (Alexa, 2009b). Xanga is primarily for blogging (text, video, or audio) and is very popular in Hong Kong.

Friendster, the first American social networking site, is extremely popular in Asia, especially in the Philippines (Alexa, 2009a). Friendster was also extremely popular in the United States until MySpace launched in 2003. MySpace offered more things to do on the site and therefore grabbed the attention of Friendster users. Friendster does not allow you to register until you say you are over 16, but that is not stopping teens from lying about their age to use it. Libraries use group pages to create communities. Patrons can join and have the library's link listed on their personal profiles in the group's section.

Bebo focuses on cultural interests such as music, authors, and videos. It is primarily used in the United Kingdom and New Zealand, but is spreading in the United States and Canada. Libraries in the UK use Bebo sites to connect with their patrons. One example is Rotorua Public Library, New Zealand (http://www.bebo.com/Profile.jsp?MemberId=4470126818). Their page is used to inform patrons of upcoming events and to explain library topics such as the Dewey Decimal system.

imeem focuses on sharing music and videos. Users share music preferences with their friends. The Middleton (WI) Public Library (http://www.imeem.com/people/0woyThl) uses imeem for teen patrons. They provide details about what the library can offer, but do not use music or video links, nor do they have any friends.

There are a variety of social networking sites that teens frequent but that do not provide a means for a library to create a community. For example, Classmates.com and MyLife (formerly Reunion.com) are used to find people who attended the same schools. Teens are already forming communities via the schools they are attending, but there is no way for a library (or school) to create a personalized page with information on either site.

Some social networking sites cater specifically to adults. Teens have a presence, but they are not encouraged to join the site, or they often lie about their age to register, so it would not be appropriate for a library to create a teen community there. Examples include fubar and Tagged. LinkedIn.com is used mainly by professionals for networking.

Forums are Web pages that allow users to create, post, and discuss their own content. Usually forums focus on a certain topic, or divide by topic, if covering many. Gaia Online is an anime-themed forum featuring a virtual world in which users create avatars, maintain homes, and play games. Yuku is another forum Web site that is popular with teens. A library could create a presence on a forum by creating a discussion on library topics. Most forums allow for a signature on each post that could include information on how to access the library for more information. However, these discussion boards are generally not the kind of place a teen would look for event news.

Today there are hundreds of social networking sites, with more launching every day. Searching the Internet for "social networking" brings up sites as they become popular. Mashable, a blog about social networking news (Sharma, 2007), has organized hundreds of social networking sites by main topic, such as books or family. Also, Wikipedia is compiling a list of social networking sites (Wikipedia contributors, 2008).

Video Sharing

Libraries can use multimedia sharing sites to post photos and videos of library events and allow patrons to comment. Posting regularly and often gives a source for news and increases excitement for events. It also creates an archive of photos for future use.

YouTube.com is the most popular multimedia sharing Web site, currently rated the fourth most-used Web site in the United States (Alexa, 2009c). YouTube allows a user to create a profile to broadcast videos. There are two levels of friendship in YouTube: subscribing and being friends. Users subscribe to receive notifications of new videos and can comment on the videos they watch. Alternatively, users can be added as a friend, which has the added benefit of being able to exchange private videos in addition to the videos posted on the profile. Users can comment on videos, which often opens a discussion. However, keep in mind that YouTube comments often are the target of spammers, so diligent moderation is needed to keep the comments ad-free.

Many libraries use YouTube. Some have posted videos about using the library and what services they offer; others have conducted contests via YouTube that solicit videos from patrons on a certain theme, such as summer reading.

Worthington (OH) Libraries has a popular YouTube site (http://youtube. com/user/worthingtonlibraries). They designed a page with a unique appearance and a variety of videos. The header is a graphic that links back to the library's Web site. They have also created playlists of themes for their videos, such as storytimes. It is even possible to post bulletins on your profile page, as Birmingham (AL) Public Library (http://www.youtube.com/user/BPLonline) has done. Bulletins are broadcast to all friends.

Other popular video sites include Hulu, Yahoo! Video (http://video.search.yahoo.com), and Google Videos (http://video.google.com).

Photo Sharing

Flickr.com is a popular social networking site that hosts photo-sharing. Users upload their own photos and link to favorites from their profile. They friend other users and then have easy access to their friends' profiles from their own main page. Flickr encourages tagging of photos and provides tag clouds for further browsing. It also encourages browsing with the Explore feature, where it finds the most interesting photos based on a complicated algorithm of ratings, comments, and views. Reading (MA) Public Library (http://www.flickr.com/photos/readingpl) has a profile where they upload photos of library happenings and allow comments.

Libraries have used the group function of Flickr to create online communities around photographs. A group allows users to become friends and to upload their own photos of a specified topic. Users are required to register to join a group so that its administrator can track who is uploading what photos and making what comments. Vancouver (Canada) Public Library (http://www.flickr.com/groups/vancouverpubliclibrary) has hundreds of photos on their Flickr group page, mostly uploaded by friends. They also sponsor a discussion forum for questions.

The Library of Congress uses Flickr to share historical photographs (http://www.loc.gov/rr/print/flickr_pilot.html). They invite users to tag and comment on the photos, including adding descriptions to enhance what is already known about the photo.

Other popular photo-sharing sites include PhotoBucket (http://photobucket.com) and Google's Picasa (http://picasaweb.google.com). These sites work in much the same way that Flickr does, so deciding which one to use is based more on personal choice and patron popularity than anything else.

Social Bookmarking Managers

Bookmark managers allow users to create a list of Web sites, which are then stored online. This allows access from any Internet-connected computer with the added benefit of being able to annotate and tag each bookmark to fit your personal needs. Then other users can browse the lists and add to their own bookmark collections. It is also possible to mark a list as private so that only the owner can see it.

The most popular social bookmarking manager is Delicious (http://deli cious.com). In addition to cataloging any bookmarks you save, it allows you to network with other users to see what they are saving. Nashville (TN) Public Library Teen Web has a Delicious account (http://delicious. com/nashpubya) that is also accessible via their Web site in tag cloud format (http://www.library.nashville.org/teens/teenweb.asp). They emphasize assignment help and good reads in their tagging.

LibraryThing (http://www.librarything.com) is a social bookmarking manager that focuses on books. Members catalog their own books, and then LibraryThing allows them to compare their lists to other members' lists. Libraries are using LibraryThing to improve access to their collections. Because each library is compared to your own, LibraryThing gives patrons a new way to look at the library's collection. Also, read-alikes are prolific, if not particularly scientific, leading a user to new books very easily. Each book gets its own profile page, which gives statistics on how many members have it in their collection, ratings, tags, recommendations of similar books, and member reviews. Members can also input "common knowledge" details such as character names, awards, publication date and place, or editors. It also provides easy links to Web sites such as Amazon and Barnes & Noble, to used book Web sites such as Abebooks and Alibris, and also to WorldCat. LibraryThing even provides an RSS feed for each title, allowing users to see any additions made to a page immediately. Washington State (WA) Library's (http://www.librarything. com/catalog/wastatelib) site displays new titles and books selected for their bibliographies and programs.

There is a very large LibraryThing group called "Librarians who LibraryThing"(http://www.librarything.com/groups/librarianswholibrar). Over 6,000 members share their personal catalogs and discuss topics in the forum. Because most of the members are librarians, the topics often cover library services as well as books.

For libraries, the real power of LibraryThing is their "Local" search. A member can input a location and find book-related places nearby. Libraries and bookstores can take advantage of this free marketing tool by adding as much information as possible to their own profile. For instance, the popular bookstore Tattered Cover in Denver, Colorado (http://www.librarything.com/venue/1947/Tattered-Cover-Book-

Store) advertises upcoming events on their profile. Members can comment on the page, add their own events, and add the profile to their favorites so that announcements appear on their main page.

In addition, LibraryThing offers a widget that users can place in a blog or on a Web site. This can be used to display titles from the cataloged books or can be used to search through the owner's LibraryThing library. Atlantic (IA) Public Library (http://www.atlantic.lib.ia.us) uses the widget to post a random selection of books from their catalog on their homepage.

LibraryThing has organizational accounts for small libraries that allow the library to use LibraryThing as their primary catalog for a nominal annual fee. Users need not register with LibraryThing to view a collection, but only account owners can make changes. Recently, LibraryThing released "LibraryThing for Libraries" (http://www.librarything.com/forlibraries), which works within a library's OPAC to display recommendations and tag clouds within the book record. The Danbury (CT) Library (http://www.danburylibrary.org) and the Bedford (TX) Public Library (http://www.lib.bedford.tx.us) currently use this product.

Library Web Pages

Your library can use social networking features to create a community for your patrons on your own Web site. By including a blog, wiki, e-mail notification, Twitter feed, or other applications on your site, you give your patrons a variety of ways to follow the library and its activities and to offer you feedback. Allowing patrons to add tags to catalog records gives yet another way to search for items that is not dependent on Library of Congress subject headings. Tagging allows the users to enable searches that are current and jargon specific.

The following is a list of suggestions to consider for your own library Web page.

Social Networking

Hennepin County (MN) Library (http://www.hclib.org) has created a social networking site within their library catalog. Patrons are asked to create a registration to post, including a photo or avatar, interests, and blog links. They can then create book lists, comment on any item in the catalog, sign up for alerts on their favorite authors, and more. Others can browse users by profile.

Ann Arbor (MI) District Library (http://www.aadl.org) is experimenting with patron-created card catalog notes. A patron is given the opportunity to add notes in handwriting fonts to the graphics of an actual card in a catalog, similar to the notes patrons wrote on real card catalog cards before computers. Also, patrons can leave reviews of a book on the catalog record, which other patrons can comment on—very similar to Amazon's review system.

Blogs

There are numerous public libraries using blogs to interact with their patrons. People can either visit the library's Web site to check for a new blog or add the library's blog to their blog reader and see new postings as they appear. Some libraries, such as Ann Arbor (MI) District Library (http://www.aadl.org), publish notices of upcoming programs and book reviews.

Allen County (IN) Public Library hosts a very graphical blog for teen patrons (http://acplteens.wordpress.com). The librarian responsible for its maintenance has posted funny and interesting videos, podcasts, and blogs about new titles by genre.

The Mosman Library of Sydney, Australia, sponsors a blog just for teen activities (http://teens.mosmanlibraryblogs.com), where teens discuss upcoming programs; share book, television, and movie reviews; and provide instructions for crafts. The blog also features pictures and information about the library and its staff.

Another Australian library, Sutherland Shire Libraries, supports blogs (http://blog.sutherlandlibrary.com) for library news and programs. They maintain multiple blogs based on various user groups—seniors, parents, students, book lovers, and local history. Many of the blog postings apply to multiple user categories and are repeated in each one.

A very complete list of library blogs, many of them specifically for teens, can be found at http://www.blogwithoutalibrary.net/links/index. php?title=Public_libraries.

RSS Feeds

It is also possible for you to create an RSS (Really Simple Syndication) feed from your library Web site. A Web feed can be set up to notify subscribers of any content changes to a certain Web page. This is useful for in-house blogs or pages that have rotating content such as programming schedules or new titles. There are quite a few free online Web feeds. A very popular one is FeedBurner (http://www.feedburner.com/fb/a/commercial).

An example of a library Web feed page is Denver (CO) Public Library's podcast site (http://podcast.denverlibrary.org). DPL gives patrons the ability to link to the library feed and be notified of new content. Another example can be found at Pepperdine University (CA) Libraries (http://library.pepperdine.edu/rss), where they have offered RSS feeds listing recently cataloged items by Library of Congress classes.

Instant Messaging

Coinciding with the phenomenon of teens engaging in digital study groups (Valeriano, 2009), more and more libraries are adding Instant Messaging (IM) to their Web pages. A 2007 study done by Knowledge Networks shows that 70 percent of teens said they send more IMs than e-mails, and 57 percent research their homework assignments while IMing. The study also found that 55 percent of the teens polled have used IM to get help with their homework, and that number grew 17 percent over the year before. Having an IM presence puts the library's name in a frequently used tool where it can be seen at a moment of need (Marketing Charts, 2007).

Meebo offers a single box IM that services all of the most popular IM programs, including Yahoo, AOL, and MSN. Most libraries use the meebome widget (http://www.meebome.com/?w), which can be placed on your Web page. Patrons click on it directly to message you or can leave a message if you are not logged in. To use the widget, you simply have to create a meebo login. Libraries using the meebome widget include the Greenfield (MA) Public Library (http://www.greenfieldpubliclibrary.org), Evanston (IL) Public Library (http://www.epl.org), and Melrose Park (IL) Public Library (http://www.melroseparklibrary.org/ask_us.htm).

Other libraries offer links to the various IM programs through which they are connected. The patron can copy the library's screen name into their own IM program. An example of this is Greene County (OH) Public Library (http://www.greenelibrary.info/Find-Answers/IM-a-Librarian.html).

Podcasts

Podcasts are audio or video recordings that you (or your teens) create to be posted online for general viewing. Audio podcasts were initially meant for downloading to an iPod, but the use of podcasting widened when posting videos became common. Whichever format you use, your podcast can be posted on a blog or social networking site or on the library's Web page. Creating a blog of mainly video podcasts is often called "vlogging" instead of "blogging." Users can download the videos to watch on their own computers or on their portable media players, such as an iPod.

Seattle (WA) Public Library's (http://www.spl.org/default.asp?page ID=audience_teens_podcast) teen podcast comprises videos of teen patrons giving book reviews and information about library events. Fairfax County (VA) Public Library has a podcast called BookCast (http://www.fairfax county.gov/library/bookcast) that features interviews with authors. North Carolina State University Libraries post podcasts (http://www.lib.ncsu. edu/podcasts) of seminars and other programs.

Wikis

A wiki is a Web site that allows users to create and edit all content. There are free wiki Web pages that anyone can use to start their own wiki. The administrator invites members at varying levels of permissions, depending on their role on the wiki. Giving "write permission" allows the user to change the content. All changes are tracked, and there is often discussion behind the page about how to improve the content.

The most famous wiki is Wikipedia.org. However, libraries are also using wikis for a variety of creative purposes. For example, Princeton (NJ) Public Library has a wiki (http://booklovers.pbwiki.com/Princeton% 20Public%20Library) where patrons and staff post book reviews. Some libraries, such as St. Joseph County (IN) Public Library (http://sjcpl.lib. in.us/subjectguides/index.php/Main_Page), have created subject guides using a wiki. They have posted both library and community information and given their librarians editing privileges. Ann Arbor (MI) District Library is hosting "Picture Ann Arbor" (http://www.aadl.org/services/products/ pictureAnnArbor), a wiki where patrons submit photos of the community that reflect everyday life. Also, many libraries use wikis for staff. WebJunction (http://webjunction.org) is "an online community for library staff" created by OCLC and funded by the Bill & Melinda Gates Foundation.

Because popularity fluctuates with the tide, the best way to decide which social networking site to use for your library is to ask your teen patrons what they like best. You can also watch which sites they frequent on library computers. Find out what they think is the best place to be, and then ask them to friend you when you are there.

WORKS CITED

Alexa. 2009a. *Top Site in Philippines.* (http://www.alexa.com/topsites/countries/ PH (accessed May 24, 2009).

Alexa. 2009b. *Traffic rankings: Orkut.com—Orkut.* http://www.alexa.com/data/details/traffic_details/orkut.com (accessed May 24, 2009).

Alexa. 2009c. *Traffic Rankings: YouTube.com—YouTube.* http://www.alexa.com/data/details/traffic_details/YouTube.com (accessed May 24, 2009).

Arrington, Michael. 2009. "Social Networking: Will Facebook overtake MySpace in 2009?" *Tech Crunch,* January 13. http://www.techcrunch.com/2009/01/13/social-networking-will-facebook-overtake-myspace-in-the-us-in-2009/ (accessed May 22, 2009).

Economist. 2007. "Social-networking mania." October 18. http://www.economist.com/business/displaystory.cfm?story_id=E1_JJJDGPV (accessed May 24, 2009).

Freiert, Max. 2008. "February top social networks—Make way for the new guys." *Compete,* March 7. http://blog.compete.com/2008/03/07/top-socialnetworks-traffic-feb-2008 (accessed May 24, 2009).

Lipsman, Andrew. 2009. "Twitter.com quadruples to 17 million U.S. visitors in last two months. *comScore,* May 12, 2009. http://blog.comscore.com/2009/05/twitter_traffic_quadruples.html (accessed May 24, 2009).

Marketing Charts. 2007. "AP-AOL instant-messaging trends survey: Mobile IM use up." *Marketing Charts,* November 15. http://www.marketingcharts.com/direct/ap-aol-instant-messaging-trends-survey-mobile-im-use-up-2399 (accessed May 24, 2009).

Sharma, Daksh. 2007. "Social networking god: 350+ social networking sites." *Mashable,* October 23. http://mashable.com/2007/10/23/social-networking-god (accessed May 24, 2009).

Simon, Mallory. 2008. "Student 'Twitters' his way out of Egyptian jail." CNN, April 25. http://www.cnn.com/2008/TECH/04/25/twitter.buck (accessed May 24, 2009).

Valeriano, Lourdes Lee. 2009. "Teen homework: It's not your mother's study group." *Business Week,* March 2. http://www.businessweek.com/careers/workingparents/blog/archives/2009/03/teen_homework_i.html (accessed May 24, 2009).

Wikipedia contributors. 2008. *List of social networking websites.* http://en.wikipedia.org/wiki/List_of_social_networking_Web sites http://en.wikipedia.org/wiki/List_of_social_networking_websites (accessed May 24, 2009).

5

◇ ◇ ◇

CONVINCING AND PLANNING: DEVELOPING YOUR LIBRARY'S WEB 2.0 PRESENCE

Kelly Czarnecki

WHY DEVELOP A SOCIAL NETWORKING PROGRAM?

Simply put, the use of social networking tools is a vital part of the lives of teens. If we want to remain relevant to teens' needs, it only makes sense that, as organizations, we need to use some of the same online tools that teens do to communicate. Sound too easy?

In 2007, Pew Internet released a report revealing that "more than half (55%) of all online American youths ages 12–17 use online social networking sites" (Lenhart and Madden, 2007). Here, *social networking* is defined as "an online place where a user can create a profile and build a personal network that connects him or her to other users."

Social networking is not just today's bandwagon or a trend that is likely to disappear anytime soon if we just "wait it out" and not make at least some effort to find out what it is all about. It has profoundly affected communication in many positive ways. In 2008 the Young Adult Library Services Association (YALSA) put together a great resource about how social networking facilitates learning related to schools and libraries. It mentions how integrating social networking as services not only helps the library remain relevant, but also models to teens safe and educational ways that social networks can be used. Who can say no to that?!

When you start to define your purpose of how using social networking as a library would benefit the organization, it will become clearer where to start. No one has the time or energy to maintain a presence on every social networking site, but chances are you are already doing things like taking photos and videos or posting news in a newsletter. If so, social networking tools can help make your job so much easier by spreading the information a lot more efficiently and effectively!

Convincing Others That It's a Good Idea

There definitely is not a one-size-fits-all approach to winning over administrators and staff in favor of developing your library's Web 2.0 presence. If only it were that easy! Often many factors have to be taken into consideration. How does the larger community feel about social networking—what do they understand about it? Are local schools using social networking? Is there a particular congressional bill originating from the town or state your library is located in regarding the issue? Does the library's free computer access attract individuals who participate in social networking activities that might be disturbing others? Do they engage in illegal activities online, such as gang activities? Is social networking to blame? It is not always easy to know where to start.

A recommended first step in getting social networking started is to take some time to educate yourself on how it is currently being used and what the various networks have to offer. One way to do that is to experiment by signing yourself up for several communities you would be interested in possibly implementing into your library. Think of it as "field research"—going out and gathering information based on your experience of being in the trenches. Be sure to try to get the perspective from those who have been using a particular social network for a while. Friend them or find another way to make that connection such as e-mail or in person. Keep in mind that sometimes we can get our toes wet in something, but it will look a whole lot different if we can make contact with those who are not the new kid on the block. Try to anticipate administrative concerns, particularly on safety issues and advertising. Do not be afraid to contact other libraries that are already using the same tools. Ask them how it came to be at their library and what, if any, roadblocks they have come upon along the way. The Library Success wiki (http://www.libsuccess.org/index.php?title=Social_Networking_

Software) is one resource to use in order to identify libraries using social networking tools.

Now, survey your library's climate regarding the previously noted questions and issues and then gauge what your plan of action might be. What is your sense of how educated your coworkers and administrators are about social networking in general, and what are their feelings about it? Working with your library's staff technology trainer (or someone in a similar position) might be a good way to begin. He or she might have an impression as to whether staff and administrators are active participants using social software.

What programs is your library currently offering to the public in terms of using Web 2.0 sites, and how is the content presented? What questions are the community members asking while in those classes? Stop in for a few minutes to gather your information. Perhaps your library does not have any classes on social networking. In that case, that might be where you start to raise community awareness and improve internal communication and knowledge about the topic. Most libraries are familiar with the 23 Things program started by Helene Blowers, formerly at the Public Library of Charlotte & Mecklenburg County, in 2006 (Blowers, 2006). Since then, hundreds of libraries and organizations across the country and overseas have adopted a program of their own to engage each other with exercises on interacting online through social networking and encouraging working together to discover information as a team.

Surveying your library's climate also extends to the larger community and informing yourself on what the critics are saying about a particular social network. Just because your base might focus on something negative about a site that you would like to use does not mean that they do not have a good point—though it might mean that the issue usually is not as simple as presented (i.e., "we'd get rid of the fear of child predators if only we got rid of all access to MySpace").

First and foremost, the library is a place for education and sharing knowledge from all sides of an issue. Perhaps organizing a panel discussion or focus group on using social networking tools, with community members from different perspectives, will help get the dialogue going. Putting together a program that can inform parents and teens about being smart citizens online—not just with MySpace, but with *all* online interactions—may go a long way toward convincing administration that the library can be a model by developing its own Web 2.0 presence.

Perhaps your library has an active core teen group such as a teen advisory board, or maybe just a regular group of teens that frequent the library.

Sometimes getting their help and using their knowledge and experience to create a library presence for you can help administration in approving the library's use of Web 2.0 tools. The Sunnyside Regional Library with the Fresno County (CA) Public Library received a grant from the California Council of the Humanities that the teen council and advisor decided to put toward filming a documentary, *Myspace Generation* (Sunnyside Teen Council of the Sunnyside Regional Library, 2006). Topics discussed include how teens use MySpace, how parents are or are not involved in their teens' use of it, how teens think of representing themselves online, and so on. The film was shown to the community, and positive dialogue ensued from the event.

Is your public library perhaps so restrictive and controlled in regard to using social networking that none of these ideas would ever fly with your administration? In the February 2008 issue of *School Library Journal*, Frances Jacobson Harris, the librarian at University High School in Illinois, wrote an article on participating in Teen Tech Week. Although the article focuses on schools, much of the one-page article applies to public libraries that might have very restricted access as well. Jacobson Harris gives several examples of where to begin and suggests that libraries "start small by picking something manageable to do and then build on a new record of success and educate administrators about the many safe and productive ways technology can be used...confront the fear-mongering with facts, figures, and concrete examples." These facts and figures could come from a number of resources, the Pew Internet and American Life Project being very helpful. Jacobson Harris also points to fear as the root cause of restrictions. Again, the fear might be coming not just from administrators, but also from other patrons who have expressed concern, and it is important that you attempt to meet everyone's needs to a certain extent. If your library does offer access to MySpace, Xanga, or Flickr, perhaps you can suggest that a committee be formed to develop talking points. Working with teens and other frequent users of these particular sites to develop this document may help both staff and administrators to feel they have something to fall back on if questioned about the use of it in the library. Also, the library can use it to promote services and programs and engage the community.

Hopefully, you are not really as alone as you might feel sometimes in convincing your library and your community that social networking is a positive tool to develop your library's presence. Check out the aforementioned Library Success wiki (www.libsuccess.org) to see which other libraries that might be similar to yours are fully immersed in a Web 2.0 presence. Do not be shy—contact them for tips on how they got started and what seemed to work for them. It does not mean the exact same path will work for you, but it cannot hurt to ask for some advice.

Also, when you think of social networking, you might tend to think only of MySpace—or feel that our administrators and community think only of it. Although it might be disappointing (to you, to your teens, and to others) that you cannot develop a presence on MySpace for the time being, focus on what you *can* do and build from there. Social networking has many possibilities, and there are other sites that your school administrators, local newspaper, after-school clubs, churches, and more might be using with success. Do not be afraid to contact them directly to get their perspectives on why they decided to participate online in a certain way, and see if they have advice on the public library doing the same. Those with a stake in the community probably share the commonality in wanting what is best for all!

The following checklist is designed to help decide which social networking site to start using, based on your library's needs and purposes. It can help you do your homework in gathering the information needed to make a case to administration for why you would like to use one site over another. Of course, using social networking to promote your library's presence does not mean you have to choose only one site. Frequently the tools work together so that you can combine several on one page, or different sites might appeal to different audiences depending on your needs and theirs. Start simple and build from there.

Questions to Ask Yourself

- How much time will a staff member or staff members be able to devote to updating the site?
- Which social networking sites are your patrons already using or talking about when they access the library?
- Whom do you want the site to target the most? Consider such things as age group and topic (books, music, videos, gaming—or all combined into one).
- What safety features are the most important to your administration and community?
- How are statistics generated by the site, and is this important to your administration?
- Do you want to highlight something in particular at your library with the social networking site (i.e., you may choose to focus on a photo-sharing site rather than a blog to highlight a visual collection)?
- How comfortable and knowledgeable are staff members as a whole in using and understanding social networking?

- What social networking sites does your local community use or not use?
- Do you want the social networking site to be primarily used internally, or for external purposes (i.e., maybe to start off with, you're seeking a better way to facilitate training and want to capture instructions on video for staff members—rather than using a video-sharing site that is open to the public)?

Hopefully this checklist will give you a better idea of how to pinpoint what it is you are looking for. You might come up with several answers and have the staff time (as well as interested users such as a teen advisory board!) to contribute to starting the site as well as maintaining it.

What to Consider

Once you have chosen your site(s) for social networking to represent the library, use the following step-by-step instructions for each to get started. Although this is not meant to be a comprehensive listing of all possible social networking sites your library could be using, the following sites were chosen because they are the ones most prevalently used by libraries, and alternative sites are listed next to the ones chosen. Chances are that most sites have similar features and share some of the same vocabulary so that you will have a better idea of what to look for when getting started with a particular tool.

Image and Video Sharing

The two sites explored are Flickr (http://www.flickr.com) and You-Tube (http://www.youtube.com). Flickr is an online photo management and sharing tool. Although an account to upload 100MB a month is free, $24.95 a year gives your library unlimited uploads and is therefore recommended. Videos can be added as well, with a limit of 90 seconds of play time per video. Some alternate photo-sharing sites that you might consider are Photobucket (http://www.photobucket.com), Picasa (http://picasa.google.com), and Smugmug (http://www.smugmug.com).

Flickr

How to Make It Useful. Aside from the obvious of uploading photos, think about some other ways to incorporate what you are already doing in ways that might reach people differently. It does not have to be a static site of photos collected from past events. Consider it as a way to promote future programs and events, or use it as the central point to collect entries for a library-run contest. Find contacts with photos that others might find interesting, such as authors or other libraries. Promote book covers, posters, and artwork through photos. Why not provide space for photo essays through flicktion (each photo is accompanied by a short descriptive fiction piece) or book/program trailers through using the video uploads? Be sure to identify your library's photo and video policy (or check into the possibilities of updating!) before deciding to use photo-sharing sites such as Flickr.

YOUR PRIVACY AND SAFETY. Information on your privacy within Flickr and Yahoo! can be found in the "Your Privacy" link at the bottom of the Flickr page (http://info.yahoo.com/privacy/us/yahoo/flickr/details. html). Flickr "Community Guidelines" and "Terms of Use" can be found here: http://www.flickr.com/guidelines.gne.
Following are a few things to note regarding your privacy:

1. You can determine who can see your photos by setting different permissions on them.
2. Under certain circumstances, Yahoo! will share your personally identifiable information with third parties. View the details here: http://help.yahoo.com/l/us/yahoo/privacy/index.html.
3. You can choose to receive notifications via e-mail when people comment on your photos and when your contacts (these are other Flickr users you can approve to be a contact) upload photos. Choose carefully because their photos will show up for other viewers as a thumbnail on your main page. You can later decide to delete contacts.
4. You can choose to form a "group." Say, for example, your library is part of a large project to which you would like others to contribute photos, such as other branches within your system. Each branch can be a member of the group and add photos. Remember that if there is more than one administrator per group, you cannot delete other administrators; they have to delete themselves. Be careful about whom you decide to add as an administrator; they can delete photos and other members, but not the group as a whole, unless they are the last administrator left of the group.

CREATING AN ACCOUNT. When you choose "create your account," you will notice that your Yahoo! ID is required. This is because Flickr is a part of Yahoo! If you do not have a Yahoo! ID, you will need to sign up for a free one. This will be your login for your Flickr account.

TAKE THE TOUR. Flickr offers an eight-step tour to find out how to get started on their site once your account is created. It is very helpful to go through this quick overview and learn how to upload photos (did you know you can use your cell phone?), edit them (get rid of red eye, add text), share them, and organize them. All great basic librarian skills can be employed in starting to build a collection! Do not forget to enlist the help of your patrons or other staff members who might be familiar with Flickr and can point out some smart suggestions.

YouTube

Compiled by Australian Librarian, Kathryn Greenhill, here is a wiki of libraries using YouTube: http://youtubeandlibraries.pbwiki.com. For everything from job recruitment to library events to staff development, it is an information-rich site. Sure, there is a lot of content that probably does not have much to do with your library, not to mention that lots of videos might not be using high-quality filming techniques. But as with most any site on the Internet, you create your niche of what to use it for and find ways that it can still be a helpful tool to promote your library— especially because it is so easy to use. YouTube is a free video-sharing site where users can upload and share videos. Some alternate video-sharing sites that you might consider are blip (http://blip.tv), or TeacherTube (http://www.teachertube.com),. When embedding YouTube videos on your library Web site (each video generates an embed code when you select it), it actually looks like it is hosted on your site and does not include YouTube's ads or other videos that might not be appropriate in close proximity to yours.

HOW TO MAKE IT USEFUL. If your library's bandwidth supports it, chances are your patrons will watch streaming video on YouTube or a similar site such as Hulu (http://www.hulu.com). Because it is a medium familiar to many and easy to use, promoting the library's programs, presenting how-tos such as using databases, and airing a recording of a visiting author or performer (with their permission of course!) are great ways to use the site. The Carnegie Library of Pittsburgh (PA) hosts a Quick Flix Teen Video Contest using YouTube where teens create videos to show why they love their library (www.clpgh.org/teens/videocontest/vote.cfm). Information Today showcases the InfoTubey Awards (www.infotubey.com), which are videos about libraries chosen for using the medium in exemplary ways. The awards are usually announced at the annual Computers in Libraries conference.

YOUR PRIVACY AND SAFETY. It is a good idea for your library's photo policy/photo release forms to include video as well. With YouTube, you can receive and accept friend invites and receive and moderate comments, as well as receive videos from others. There is a safety link on YouTube (http://www.youtube.com/t/safety) that talks about everything from what seems like common sense—such as not posting information in a video you would not want others to know about—to marking your personal videos private. The YouTube privacy notice (http://www.youtube.com/t/privacy) talks about what the company does with your personal information and what information is publicly available to others when you sign up for an account.

CREATING AN ACCOUNT. When signing up for your account, you are asked for an e-mail address, password, username, location (including country and zip code), birth date, and gender. You are reminded that you cannot upload material that you do not own or that is a copyright violation.

TAKE THE TOUR. YouTube has a helpful forums board with contributions from other users as well as troubleshooting tips and how-to videos for navigating their site. In addition, some useful features of the site include something called TestTube, where you can add commentary and notes to your videos, remix and add music to them, watch a video on a mobile device such as a cell phone, or subscribe to the RSS feed so that you can automatically be informed when a video is uploaded. The commentary feature is a great way to provide information on how a video was made for others who want to create something similar.

Blogs and Social Networking Sites

The library can build virtual environments for teens by creating a presence on an online space that is already popular with many teens that you serve. For example, if Facebook is commonly accessed rather than Xanga, that might be a good place for the library to start. Deciding why a library would want to have a presence on such a site in the first place is one of the first questions you'll need to answer before adding content to it.

How do you even begin to decide what site to populate? For starters, sites such as MySpace (http://www.myspace.com) and Facebook (http://www.facebook.com) are often used to connect with others based on interests such as books, music, writing, movies, cooking, and exercising. For pretty much anything that someone has an interest in and wants to connect with others over, other similar people can be found. In this context, it makes perfect sense for a library to come on board. By setting up a virtual presence in a space that is already a comfortable place for teens to be who they are, the library is saying they value being in places where teens can feel better about themselves. They can also create opportunities online for teens to visit the library by sharing about upcoming programs or having a discussion based on the amount of comments received when posting about something that resonated with a lot of people.

WordPress (http://www.wordpress.com) and Blogger (http://www.blogger.com) are two well-known sites used by libraries to connect with teens through writing. By enabling teens to comment on the posts (or better yet, create posts themselves), they can become more articulate in expressing their opinions and feeling comfortable with what those ideas are. "Blogs present a great opportunity for supporting teens in their understanding of the world beyond me," states Linda Braun in *Teens, Technology, and Literacy; Or, Why Bad Grammar Isn't Always Bad* (2006). In other words, a library's presence on a blog successfully models the use of a virtual space in a way that moves beyond being about someone's personal life (even though there is certainly without question a place for that). This puts it into the broader public realm of expressing oneself on behalf of an organization and appealing to a wide range of people and interests.

Here are some snapshot descriptions of the just-discussed sites.

Social Circles

MySpace

There is probably no social networking site that has been more talked about than MySpace, which was launched in 2003. Although it was originally a place where indie bands got to showcase their music and share with others, it has grown to be much more. Although we might be most familiar with the dark side of MySpace—people meeting strangers online and then in real life only to face a tragic ending, or being bullied anonymously by others—many libraries still have a presence on MySpace and for good reason. Looking at the appeal to teens, according to danah boyd, MySpace is attractive to youth because dealing with popularity and jockeying for social status are related to friending. Leaving comments, posting photos, and having profiles is a combination of all of this, where MySpace "provides an opportunity to craft the intended expression through language, imagery and media," states boyd in *Identity Production in a Networked Culture: Why Youth Heart MySpace* (boyd, 2006).

How to Make It Useful. Since there has been so much controversy with MySpace, why would a library even want to consider having a presence there? YALSA's (2008) aforementioned resource, a social networking toolkit for school and public libraries, gives resources for educating the community and its teens and talks about how social networking facilitates learning in both schools and libraries. In regard to MySpace, the document points out examples of libraries using it for patron access to the library catalog and research tools, to provide information on programs and services. It also explains how teens who are not traditional library users are attracted to this online space because they are already familiar and comfortable with the technology.

Even if the stories that we hear on the news about MySpace are mostly negative, there are many people (and not just libraries) using the site for positive reasons. "Authors, librarians, and educators are now using MySpace as a way to build community with their readers and with their users," states Linda Braun (2006). Building community and reaching nontraditional users is definitely at the core of what libraries are about. An appealing feature of MySpace is that not only does it incorporate blogging, but also video, photo albums, music, instant messaging, and commenting are all great ways to incorporate what libraries are already doing with media creation and teens.

For a list of libraries using MySpace and Facebook, visit the Library Success wiki here: http://tinyurl.com/43bbrm.

Your Privacy and Safety. MySpace may not be for every library, and that's okay, because there are plenty of other social networking sites out there. However, if your teens are heavy users of MySpace, perhaps organizing classes and workshops around safety while simultaneously launching the library's presence online will serve as a preventive measure and counteract negative backlash. Being a model of responsible use of the site and friending teens who use the library can be a great way to create one more safe place online for teens to reach out to and connect with one another. MySpace has made a lot of improvements to their site as far as safety measures are concerned since they first started in 2003, including such things as deleting thousands of profiles of sex offenders and making the default profile setting "private" for minors (ages 13–17). More improvements will likely be made by the time this book is published as well.

Your first step in establishing your library's presence on MySpace and being a positive role model is to represent yourself professionally with photos, music, video, blog posts, and more. This might seem like common sense, but sometimes we get so comfortable with a medium that we might forget. Having an image of the library as the profile photo serves as a reminder that this is the organization's Web site and not a personal space for whatever staff maintains and updates the site. Such a neutral presence might also help to bring more staff into updating the site, knowing they can do so anonymously. To keep your site interesting to teens and other library users, you might want all the staff help you can get! MySpace addresses safety at the bottom and top of their page here: http://tinyurl.com/6cwkoa, including videos on profile settings as well as featured tips and reminders such as "Your profile and MySpace forums are public spaces." The site's privacy policy, regarding what the company does with personally identifiable information, is listed here: http://tinyurl.com/25g85z.

CREATING AN ACCOUNT. MySpace is intended for ages 13 and over. Information that is required when someone signs up includes e-mail, password, and first and last name (people are reminded to give their real name if they want friends to be able to search for them; otherwise, that information is kept private). Country, city, and zip code follow, again reminding people to list their correct zip code if they want friends to find them. You can choose whether to have your birthday visible by checking a box. In order to process the sign up, you are required to check a box that indicates you agree with the terms of service (http://tinyurl.com/2paova) and privacy policy (http://tinyurl.com/25g85z). Next, users are asked to upload a photo as an optional step and are reminded of MySpace's photo policy (http://tinyurl.com/5fnws7), which basically says that MySpace has the right to remove any photos if they include copyrighted or indecent material and personally identifiable information. Adding friends from your Gmail address book is a possibility as well. Aside from verifying your e-mail address, that is all the information you need to create an account. Including videos, photos, friends, music, and backgrounds are all optional and fun things the subscriber will want to do next. Updating the profile, which contains likes and dislikes of music, television, books, and more, is where users can add information about themselves.

In 2007, teen librarian Jesse Vieau and technology education librarian Matt Gullett, with ImaginOn, of the Public Library of Charlotte & Mecklenburg County, developed a MySpace-for-parents class with accompanying booklet (http://tinyurl.com/5ejjlx). It is a helpful tool in terms of setting up an account and what your profile should (and should not) say about you. General interaction tips such as commenting and adding photos are included as well. Finally, resources including safety tips and responsible Internet use are listed.

TAKE THE TOUR. MySpace offers a quick tour in both English and Spanish here: http://tinyurl.com/66hcjg. It is self-paced, allowing the visitor to click through links and view screen shots, and divided into three categories: "MySpace is a place for friends," "MySpace is Your Space," and "MySpace keeps you connected." A button at the end of each page encourages the viewer to sign up for an account. Interestingly, nothing on safety and exercising good judgment is included in this section.

Facebook

HOW TO MAKE IT USEFUL. Although it varies from one community to the next, Facebook is gaining popularity among its young users. It does not share the well-known controversy of MySpace yet still offers many of the same features. Distance-learning librarian Meredith Farkas recommends using Facebook as a professional development tool, thinking of it as a collection of experts (2007). Although as professionals we would probably have our own Facebook accounts, separate from the one that is chosen to represent the library, it is also good to think about a library Facebook presence in terms of modeling it for teens as the face that represents the library online. For example, you might write a post about how your library just got the new copy of Stephenie Meyer's latest book. You might then receive a response back about how someone knows of a *Breaking Dawn* party in town. What a great professional contact—see if the party hosts are on Facebook and help spread the word!

Hennepin County (MN) Library provides a great example of how to use Facebook (http://tinyurl.com/484jkn) and incorporate reference service with librarians by embedding a chat widget, listing their address and main library Web site, as well as embedding their catalog as a widget so that people can search the library without leaving Facebook.

YOUR PRIVACY AND SAFETY. Anyone 13 and older is eligible to sign up for an account. Terms of use are located here: http://www.facebook.com/terms.php; the company's privacy policy is here: http://www.facebook.com/policy.php. Facebook has improved its security measures, especially in regard to younger users since it came out in 2004, a year after the launch of MySpace. For example, inappropriate content is flagged or removed, and when personal information is shared, warning messages appear on the site. One of the greatest safety features of the site is that profile pages where people's information exists cannot be accessed unless that person is added as a friend. Although it is easy to add someone, at least it is a safety device and up to the person who created an account to decide whether to add another as a friend or not.

CREATING AN ACCOUNT. Your real name and e-mail is required to sign up for an account. Through privacy settings, you can limit what people can see on your page. Your birth date and password are required as well. If using Facebook to represent the library, then the library's Web site address, hours, interests based on the population you think the space will attract, and so on is all appropriate information to keep as part of your profile.

TAKE THE TOUR. Under the "help" link at the bottom of Facebook's site is a Getting Started Guide. Here you are instructed on how to find friends, classmates, or coworkers (without having signed up for an account). Next, how to set up a profile and edit it is explained. Information on putting contact info, such as a cell phone number or e-mail address, into a profile is described in the context of the user having control over who sees that information (i.e., those who are friended by the user). Finally, "Explore Facebook" talks about connecting with others through joining a network, viewing friends' profiles, and starting a discussion with a group that has similar interests. By now, ideas for how the library can be involved are probably churning away!

Blogs

WordPress

HOW TO MAKE IT USEFUL. WordPress is a free blog-publishing platform that has many of the statistical gathering tools that are often attractive to libraries in terms of tracking programs and visits to the physical library. These tools include counting the number of visitors to the blog, identifying search words used on the blog, and tracking links that refer to the blog. The North Plains Public Library in Oregon uses WordPress (http://nplibrary.org), as does the Stevens Memorial Library in Massachusetts (http://www.stevensmemlib.org), which gives their sites a very clean interface and blog-like entries where expanded text can be read on another page without cluttering up the main one.

The Carnegie Library of Pittsburgh (PA) (http://clpteensburgh.word press.com) uses their blog for teens. Organizations related to libraries, such as StoryCorps® (http://www.storycorps.net), use it as well. Evanston (IL) Public Library uses WordPress for their teen space, the Virtual Loft (http://eplteen.wordpress.com). The reason for its appeal is that posts are archived by date and searchable, a feature that static Web pages cannot incorporate as easily. Posts are tagged, enabling them to be searched or browsed via common key words that are used to summarize the post. The author of the post is viewable, and a link is given that allows you to contact them. Readers can interact with the post by leaving comments.

Libraries that effectively use WordPress keep the information updated as well as use it for two-way communication and have results from patrons communicating through comments to prove it.

YOUR PRIVACY AND SAFETY. WordPress's privacy policy can be found here: http://automattic.com/privacy. They state, "We don't ask you for personal information unless we truly need it," which is different from a few of the other sites mentioned so far. WordPress gives the option of having private as well as public blogs. If you want only invited guests to see your content or want to have certain posts within a public blog marked as private, that is possible. WordPress uses Akismet for blocking spammers from leaving unwanted comments on your blog. Uploading videos and photos, adding sidebar widgets from Meebo for instant-messaging chat (great reference tool!), using the Delicious bookmarking site, and more are all really easy. This is a great reminder to not post anything you would not want everyone else to know about.

CREATING AN ACCOUNT. WordPress requires the user to fill out a one-step form with a username, which does not have to be the real name of the person, and password. A real e-mail address is required because you will have to click on a link within the message sent from WordPress in order to activate your account. You need to check that you agree to the terms of service that can be found here: http://wordpress.com/tos. Voila—you are ready to name your blog and get started!

TAKE THE TOUR. WordPress does not take a lot of training to set up. There are great tutorials (http://codex.wordpress.org/WordPress_Lessons) that cover everything from getting started with the platform as a beginner to design, features, and functions of WordPress. In the section on how to administer your blog, you can find out how to do such things as add users, enable or disable comments, manage posts, and troubleshoot as well. An FAQ list is also included, and readers are encouraged to check that for their answers before submitting a question. In March of 2008, a video was added to YouTube for a "behind the scenes" instruction on using Word-Press: http://tinyurl.com/5bn9b3. Although WordPress has come out with additional versions since the video was made, it is very step-by-step and still helpful in leading the novice through setting up a presence on WordPress.

Blogger

How to Make It Useful. Blogger is a free and commonly used site to instantly create a blog in just a few easy steps. Complete with instructions, templates, and a user-friendly help menu, you can publish your thoughts in no time. Launched in the year 2000, Blogger was acquired by Google in 2003. This takeover allowed those with Blogger accounts and users of the Google toolbar to directly post by clicking on "BlogThis!" links within Google. Also, the photo-editing and photo-management site Picasa (http://picasa.google.com) was integrated into Blogger as well. The Carnegie Library of Pittsburgh (PA) uses Blogger and makes it almost look more like MySpace (http://clpteens.blogspot.com). Widgets for voting, music, and a "skin" or background are all part of the picture that will attract teens. The Hillsborough County (FL) Public Library Cooperative uses it to showcase pictures from events, recommend books, and let readers know what is in the collection (http://hcplcteens.blogspot.com). Olson Middle School in Minnesota uses Blogger to recommend and review books (http://omsbook blog.blogspot.com). For a list of public and school libraries that blog, visit the Blogging Libraries Wiki here: http://tinyurl.com/pvzvp. Several links on the site are dead or lead to blogs no longer being used, but the wiki still gives a good overview of how many organizations are using WordPress, Blogger, Edublogs, and other platforms. Also, most of the blogs, though aimed at teens, do not appear to have a lot of interactive dialogue between the readers and the writers; overall, it appears to be mostly one-way communication. That certainly does not mean that no one is reading the blogs, but interactivity is important in being able to create a community online.

Your Privacy and Safety. Blogger's privacy notice can be found here: http://www.blogger.com/privacy. Google reminds bloggers that profile information such as photos, birthdays, or location can be edited at any time. Their content policy is listed here: http://www.blogger.com/content.g. Although users are encouraged to enact free speech, they are also reminded of the boundaries, including no pornography, hateful or violent content, or copyright infringement. You can choose to enable or delete comments, be found from your profile information listed (or not), and decide whom you want to read and/or write to your blog, as well as decide to keep some spaces private and viewable to only whom you allow.

CREATING AN ACCOUNT. As their site says, a blog can be created in three easy steps. Because Blogger is aligned with Google, a valid Gmail address is needed to sign up, which can be acquired at http://mail.google.com. A password, a display name that you want others to see, and acceptance of the terms of service are also required (http://www.blogger.com/terms.g). The name of the blog is then chosen, a template or design is picked, and you are ready to get started with your blog.

TAKE THE TOUR. The Blogger tour (http://www.blogger.com/tour_start.g) covers the very basics of blogging and how to get started. It takes readers through a simple process of answering the question, "What is a blog?" and shows how Blogger can help people use it for what they want. Some of its features are discussed as well, such as adding photos and blogging while mobile via cell phone. The tour is definitely helpful for the novice blogger, but if you are looking for something more advanced, such as how to edit your Blogger template design and add video, podcasts, RSS feeds, and so on, you may want to check out the Blogger Help menu here: http://help.blogger.com.

Virtual Worlds

Second Life

HOW TO MAKE IT USEFUL. Most libraries using Second Life (http://www.secondlife.com) are located in what is called the main grid (mg), which is a space for those 18 and over. And most are located in what is called InfoIsland, which is a connection of islands. Each island (or sim) is the equivalent of a little over 16 acres. There are over 400 librarians working as volunteers on the main grid. Some of the services they provide include informational displays, reference, concerts, book discussions, and immersive historical environments from books or certain time periods. There are also several libraries on what is called the teen grid (tg), but most of them are private.

Private means that the owner of the island can strictly control who enters their space. The teen grid is completely separate from the main grid, and anyone 18 and over is required to get a background check before accessing it. Ramapo Islands, which is based in Suffern, New York, in real life, is on the teen grid and run by school media specialist Peg Sheehy (http://

ramapoislands.edublogs.org). She uses her islands as a way for teachers to connect with students in every subject from history, language arts, and English as a second language to math, music, and more. She posts notices on the blog about the events the students participate in, as well as their reactions to using the virtual medium to learn.

Eye4You Alliance Island is run by Kelly Czarnecki from the Public Library of Charlotte & Mecklenburg County (http://eye4youalliance. youthtech.info). It is used to showcase history and science to teens in a fun way. Rather than being a place for reference service or book discussions, Eye4You is a place for teens to create. Partners such as NASA run robot-building contests, Science Friday radio streams from NPR, and teachers and librarians volunteer their time to run Model UN discussions; some teachers bring their classes (computer classes, after-school clubs) to the island, and the teens run their own projects and events as well, such as journalistic reporting on what is happening on the grid, building contests, or meetings. The Topeka and Shawnee County (KS) Public Library (http://www.tscpl.org/teens/section/second_lifers) runs a club called the Second Lifers where teens are able to meet twice a week at the library or virtually on their island, called Oz, and participate in various events. Oz is a private island on the teen grid. The island's activities are coordinated by librarian Jean Gardner.

YOUR PRIVACY AND SAFETY. If you own a space on Second Life's main grid or teen grid, you have the option for it to be a private and thus control who is on the island. Island fees are listed here: http://secondlife. com/land/purchasing.php. There are monthly maintenance fees that pay for such things as server space and upkeep, and they range from about $75 USD to $295 USD. If you do not wish to have a private sim, you can opt for a public one and allow anyone access. If you are the owner, or the owner gives you privileges, you can ban avatars (digital representations of real people) that are behaving inappropriately. Examples of inappropriate behavior might include verbal harassment, "object griefing" such as leaving objects around the island, or pestering another avatar by following the avatar around. Teens have instant access to the Lindens, who are the employees of the company. They (and approved adults) can file what is called an abuse report, documenting the incident with text and a photo. The avatar can then be banned by the Lindens or the estate owner. The Second Life community itself, especially on the teen grid, is self-policed, and it is unlikely that someone creating a disturbance will get away with it for long.

CREATING AN ACCOUNT. If you are creating an account for the main grid, you can sign up for a free membership here: http://tinyurl.com/6rb468. You will choose an avatar's first and last name (which does not have to be your real name) and then fill out your e-mail address, gender, and birth date and confirm that you agree to the terms of service (http://secondlife.com/corporate/tos.php). If you want to be on the teen grid as an adult, you need to be affiliated with a project first or purchase your own island. A list of projects so far on the teen grid can be found on this wiki: http://tinyurl.com/2qlenn. Contacting the owner of that project and then finding out if your ideas match what they are looking for is how you can begin to get affiliated with something already occurring on the teen grid. You will also need a background check here: https://www.ascertainsi.com/secondlife/bgConsent.asp. You sign up for an account the same way you would for the main grid. The estate owner for the teen grid then contacts Linden Lab and requests that your avatar be moved over to their estate on the teen grid. Once you are on the teen grid, as an approved adult, you are locked to your island and not able to teleport to other islands without creating an entirely new avatar and getting the estate owner's permission to be involved on their island as well.

System requirements to run Second Life on Windows, Mac, and Linux can be found here: http://secondlife.com/support/sysreqs.php.

TAKE THE TOUR. This video, a bit over three and a half minutes long, will show you how to sign up for an account in Second Life, log on, and navigate around an island: http://www.youtube.com/watch?v=dud0Oe9n3FA. The "What is Second Life?" link from the company's main site will take the viewer through the different aspects of the virtual world (http://secondlife.com/whatis).

SmallWorlds

HOW TO MAKE IT USEFUL. SmallWorlds runs inside your Web browser and was launched in June 2008. It requires Javascript to be enabled and the latest Adobe Flash Player as well. Users create rooms, design their avatar, and interact through text chat. Content is not user-generated, but it can be imported from such social networking sites as Flickr, YouTube, Twitter, and Last.fm (for music; http://www.last.fm.com). As the SmallWorlds site says, "Web 2.0 meets Web 3.D. However, unlike watching or listening to media on your computer by yourself, SmallWorlds uses its *Social Interplay Engine* to enable you and your friends to experience your favorite videos, music, images and widgets, together—in real-time" (http://blog.smallworlds. com). The space is not being widely used by libraries but might be another great way to integrate content the library is already using through various social networking sites into an immersive environment that avatars can experience in real time and through chat. Another large component of SmallWorlds is game play, where members can play games and earn coins to help furnish their rooms. The games often teach the user how to understand the virtual world more by seeing what it has to offer.

YOUR PRIVACY AND SAFETY. In regard to your personal information, the company's privacy policy can be found at http://www.smallworlds. com/privacy-policy/. Members can be invited to visit your room, and you can determine who, if anyone, will be allowed to decorate your room as well. The terms of service are available at http://www.smallworlds. com/terms-of-service/. If you click on "account settings" in the bottom left of the screen, you can choose the obscenity filter, which will block obscene words from text. Do not let this fool you, though—there are a lot of ways to type around an obscenity filter!

CREATING AN ACCOUNT. The first step in creating an account is to pick and customize an avatar, choosing the hair, clothes, and other accessories as well as a name and dance moves. Next you can register your details, including an e-mail and password, if you would like to return again with that same avatar.

TAKE THE TOUR. Located on the main page is a link to take the tour of the site (http://www.smallworlds.com/login.php). The forum board (http:// forum.smallworlds.com), help and support (http://www.smallworlds. com/help-support/), and frequently asked questions (http://www.small worlds.com/faq/) are great resources as well.

Wikis

A wiki is a set of Web pages that can be edited by those given permission to do so (which could range from one person to everyone) and modified by authorized users with html. This differs from a blog, where comments can be made by everyone if this feature is enabled, but the post itself cannot be modified unless you are the blog's owner or have given other people permissions to do so. Using html to edit a wiki does not require advanced knowledge of this computer language. Knowing how to make a hyper-link, insert images, and create breaks in lines or bolded text are some of the basic skills that are needed and can be quickly picked up.

How to Make It Useful. According to the PALINET Leadership network (http://pln.palinet.org/wiki/index.php/Wikis_and_libraries), a few reasons you should care about wikis are the following: they can provide key collaborative resources; they can be used as staff-only sources, such as reference wikis or community wikis; and many patrons are already using wikis, especially Wikipedia.

Your Privacy and Safety. Privacy and safety in relation to wikis revolve mostly around the permissions you want to give people to view and/or modify your content. The nature of a wiki is to collaborate and share with others. Yet if you do not take precautions to install spam filters, or if you open it up for the entire world to edit without having some of the pages locked or without maintaining a backup, you could be in for a whole lot of heartache.

In the general area of your wiki, you will find information on assigning permissions and on how to give the desired level of control to another person. MediaWiki's permission instruction page can be found here: http://www.mediawiki.org/wiki/Help:Assigning_permissions. The WikiMatrix (http://www.wikimatrix.org) is a resource that has compiled wikis and compares them in over one hundred areas, including the cost, the operating system it runs on, and whether it offers themes and skins.

Creating an Account. Most wikis offer a range of services. Many are free, but cost can be involved for such things as storage space, custom domain name, or backup files. You will have to decide for yourself what you will need. If you are using the wiki for internal purposes, a specific domain name probably is not all that important. You can always expand if the uses of your wiki grow from what you originally anticipated.

Taking the Tour. Many companies offer a video demonstration of what their wiki can do for you. To find out which libraries are using what wikis and for which purpose, view the Library Success wiki here: http://www.libsuccess.org/index.php?title=Main_Page. PBwiki is commonly used, and their videos can be viewed at http://vodpod.com/tag/pbwiki. Another great resource that will give information on how wikis work and how libraries are using them with patrons as well as internally is the Five Weeks to a Social Library course on wikis http://www.sociallibraries.com/course/week3.

PREVENTING ABUSE

At the beginning of this chapter, it was mentioned that one of the reasons for establishing a presence on a social networking site was to model safe, responsible, and educational use. That is a great preventive measure to take against those wanting to abuse your site. For example, filtering your comments before they even appear on the site shows others that you know what you are doing and cannot just be pushed around and caught off-guard.

One of the important things to remember about bullying is that even though it can feel a lot more frightening online if someone is leaving you mean comments, such behavior did not start with the Internet. When people are anonymous, they often say harsher or more outrageous things than they might to your face. Unfortunately, bullying has been around for a long time, and it still exists in many ways, including online. Having the tools and the knowledge to combat a different form of bullying is important and not impossible.

Talking to teens about how they use social networking in safe and responsible ways might give you some good ideas to implement for the library's presence. You might even find that teens are indeed having these kinds of conversations with their parents, who are also helping them use the sites safely and responsibly.

A great resource for using social networking in a respectful way toward others is Nancy Willard's book, *Cyber-Safe Kids, Cyber-Savvy Teens: Helping Young People Learn to Use the Internet Safely and Responsibly* (2007). According to the biography on her book, Willard is an educator, lawyer, educational technology consultant, and mom. Although the dialogue is directed mostly toward parent–child communication, the lessons are also relevant to organizations setting up a social networking presence, such as libraries. One of the most helpful aspects of her book is that she breaks down specifically what the risks and concerns are in a non-scary way and separates fact from fiction. Willard asserts that online communities are "a natural progression of Internet information and communications technologies. They are attractive to teens and they are here to stay. Parents simply must pay attention to the need to ensure that their children have the knowledge, skills, and values to make safe and responsible choices on these sites." Some of her recommendations include making it your business to know what your child is doing online, providing "teachable moments" to your child when viewing their online activities, and installing monitoring software if your child has exhibited inappropriate online behavior.

Another author who helps put into perspective what is happening online is YPulse (http://www.ypulse.com) blogger Anastasia Goodstein, who wrote *Totally Wired: What Teens and Tweens are Really Doing Online* (2007). "The good news is that what teens are doing online and with cell phones and other devices doesn't have to keep you up at night any more than what they may be doing at the mall or their friend's houses or wherever they hang out offline." One of the best things Goodstein does in this book is put into perspective how social networking and developing an identity online are similar to many things we did as teenagers, such as talk on the phone or decorate our room with posters. If a teen's offline behaviors indicate that they are isolating themselves from family and friends, or their grades are changing as a result of being online too much, it is a sign that an investigation into the child's behavior is needed.

Although complete safety online is not 100 percent possible, neither is safety offline. We can all do the best that we can and be models for those that use social networking as part of their daily lives. As librarians, we can make sure that our library's Internet policy is updated and visible online for all to see.

WORKS CITED

Blowers, Helen. 2006. *Learning 2.0*, May 2. http://plcmcl2-about.blogspot.com (accessed May 24, 2009).

boyd, danah. 2006. *Identity Production in a Networked Culture: Why Youth Heart MySpace*. http://danah.org/papers/AAAS2006.html (accessed May 24, 2009).

Braun, Linda. 2006. *Teens, Technology, and Literacy: Or, Why Bad Grammar Isn't Always Bad*. Westport, CT: Libraries Unlimited.

Farkas, Meredith. 2007. *Social Software in Libraries: Building Collaboration, Communication, and Community Online*. Medford, NJ: Information Today, Inc.

Goodstein, Anastasia. 2007. *Totally Wired: What Teens and Tweens Are Really Doing Online*. New York: Saint Martin's Griffin.

Harris, Frances Jacobson. 2008. "Teen tech week, despite limited access." *School Library Journal* 54 (2): 20.

Lenhart, Amanda, and Mary Madden. 2007. *Social Networking Websites and Teens: An Overview*. Pew Internet, January 7. http://www.pewinternet.org/Reports/2007/Social-Networking-Websites-and-Teens.aspx (accessed May 24, 2009).

Sunnyside Teen Council of the Sunnyside Regional Library (CA). 2006. *Myspace Generation,* December 6. http://www.youtube.com/watch?v=t0iXNDESaJk (accessed May 24, 2009).

Willard, Nancy. 2007. *Cyber-Safe Kids, Cyber-Savvy Teens: Helping Young People Learn to Use the Internet Safely and Responsibly.* San Francisco: Jossey-Bass.

Young Adult Library Services Association. 2008. "Teens & social networking in school and public libraries: A toolkit for librarians & library workers." Young Adult Library Services Association. http://www.ila.org/netsafe/SocialNetworkingToolkit.pdf (accessed May 27, 2009).

6

◇ ◇ ◇

NOW LET'S USE IT: CREATIVE PROGRAMMING

Robyn M. Lupa

Social networking lends itself to a multitude of programming possibilities. An excellent way to get started is during Teen Tech Week, sponsored by the Young Adult Library Services Association (YALSA) every March. YALSA's Web page has abundant resources, research, and ideas, including "Tech Guides" that tell you how to make music with teens; how to develop programming with virtual worlds, useful applications for blogs, wikis, and RSS; tips on planning gaming programs; and the nuts and bolts of podcasting. The Teen Tech Week is a foundation to get you started applying Web 2.0 technologies for entertaining and educational programming in your public library! (http://www.ala.org/ala/mgrps/divs/yalsa/teen techweek/ttw08/ttw.cfm)

Austin (TX) Public Library's collaboration with other agencies has enabled them to give the kids of Central Texas access to technology resources, aiding Austin's reputation as one of the most wired communities in the country. Wired for Youth staff educate and train kids on a wide variety of technology topics. Their "Tech-Know" Web site is an excellent resource for anyone— teens, librarians and educators—to learn how to delve into Web design as well as image and photo manipulation (http://www.wiredforyouth.com/ tech.cfm). Use these sites to host tutorials at your library or have confidently wired teens teach classes to newbies.

Following are some other ideas for inspiration.

BLOGS

Set up blogs for creative writing and book sharing—then host face-to-face receptions periodically so that the teens who contribute and remark on each other's works can meet. Link to author's sites so that teens can follow—and interact with—favorites. Some popular authors with thriving blogs include the following:

- Laurie Halse Anderson, http://halseanderson.livejournal.com
- Holly Black, http://blackholly.livejournal.com
- Meg Cabot, http://megcabot.com/diary
- Sarah Dessen, http://writergrl.livejournal.com
- Rachel Cohn, http://www.myspace.com/rachel_cohn
- Alex Flinn, http://www.alexflinn.com
- Neil Gaiman, http://journal.neilgaiman.com
- Gail Giles, http://notjazz.livejournal.com
- John Green, http://www.sparksflyup.com/weblog.php
- Megan McCafferty, http://www.meganmccafferty.com/retro blogger
- Scott Westerfeld, http://scottwesterfeld.com/blog

Go to the TeenLibWiki for many more authors who maintain blogs, as well as a list of those with MySpace pages (http://yalibrarian.com/yalib_wiki/index.php?title=Main_Page).

Although some teens may still have traditional pen-and-paper diaries, millions have taken to online journaling. Whereas diaries from the past were private, teen bloggers willingly share their thoughts with many others. They can decorate pages with colorful wallpaper, borders, font, and background music and post anywhere from just a few lines to pages of text. One's "current mood" is defined with text and a graphic as well as a song of the moment (complete with the ability to click on the tune and hear it, with album cover art). Readers can then post comments on that specific entry, creating a dialogue with the writer and with each other.

LiveJournal (http://www.livejournal.com), Xanga (http://www.xanga.com), and Blogger (http://www.blogger.com) are popular blog sites. Teens can limit who may view their blog and/or respond to it. Invite a writing teacher in to help brainstorm ideas on how young writers can get started—observations about the world, inner thoughts, or critical reviews of books, movies, and music. Conversely, get kids who are actively journaling online to break away from the keyboard and try it with pen and paper. Buy supplies to enable them to decorate a print journal. Have them write and then compare and contrast the experience of being online and the old-fashioned method. You can take this opportunity to remind teens that, despite perceived anonymity, their blogs are public, anyone may access them, and they might want to think twice about some content.

Host a mock-Printz (or Oscars or Grammys, etc.) awards using a blog. Discussions of nominees can become lively as followers express their opinions by posting comments. Allen County (IN) Public Library provides a good example of the use of a blog for a virtual mock awards program: http://acplmockprintz.wordpress.com.

Post teen advisory board (TAB) meeting minutes and updates on a blog for members to readily access and contribute to. Multnomah County (OR) Library uses their teen blog for Teen Council information and much more (http://teens.multcolib.org/blog/teens).

To help you get started with the use of blogs, peruse this list for many more public library blog examples: http://www.blogwithoutalibrary.net/links/index.php?title=Public_libraries.

PHOTOS AND VIDEO

Host Flickr contests in which teens post their photos on a designated area of the library's Web site. Allow others to comment and vote on what they consider to be the best. Tie this into other art and photography workshops that you offer. The Oakland Public Library (CA) took photos of their teen manga contest submissions and put them on Flickr for friends and family to view (http://www.flickr.com/photos/opl_main_teen/sets/72157604473031963).

Similarly, plan a workshop with inexpensive camcorders and editing using Adobe. Have teens post their creations for critical peers to view—and add the video links to their own MySpace or Facebook pages. Buy some snacks and watch the videos in your meeting room on a big screen. Challenge teens to create films on specific topics: advertise your summer reading club or publicize Teen Read Week. Show some creative examples before getting started: see Allen County's amusing summer promotion (http://www.youtube.com/watch?v=_7BYiVRUHfw), Florida high school students' participation in a contest to create a PSA for their library's chat reference service (http://www.tblc.org/aal/directorschair), and the Denver (CO) Public

Library's "How I have fun at the library" video contest (http://teens.denver
library.org/media/youtube.html) in which winners were awarded MP3
players. Niles (IL) Public Library District has their own site on YouTube
containing "videos created by and for teens" (http://www.youtube.com/
nilespubliclibrary). Finally, take a look at Worthington (OH) Libraries'
impressive "Programs *to Go*" site (http://www2.worthingtonlibraries.org/
programs2go), which contains video and audio for all ages, ranging from
children's storytimes and teen readers theater to a Q&A with author John
Green to developing a career plan. Patrons may comment on and interact
with one another by posting their thoughts on YouTube.

Book trailers are some of the most creative outlets available for teens.
Once a book is selected, allow them to gather in a meeting room to ham-
mer out a script—whether it is acting out an overview of the novel,
portraying one scene, or devising a music video about it. Mark Geary
offers a tutorial on how to get started with free downloadable software if
video cameras are not readily available: http://www.techlearning.com/
article/8160.

PODCASTING

Use podcasting for book talks and readers' advisory (first, brief yourself
on legal guidelines by referring to this comprehensive site: http://wiki.
creativecommons.org/Podcasting_Legal_Guide). Get a group of teens to
put together read-alike lists for popular genres, and then book-talk them
and post the podcasts on the library's Teen Pages, Facebook page, and
MySpace. See Public Library of Charlotte and Mecklenburg County's (NC)
site for outstanding ideas (http://www.plcmc.org/readers_club) as well
as the creations of New Hampshire's Hopkinton High School and Middle
School librarians (http://www.hopkintonschools.org/hhs/library/pod
cast.html#anchor823756).

A practical and relevant program to offer teens is on the topic of prep-
ping and navigating options for higher education. Invite college recruiters
or counselors into the library for real-time programs. But being aware of
the low attendance many young adult programs receive because of con-
flicting schedules, inadequate advertising, jobs, and homework, you can
now preserve the program virtually by turning it into a podcast, as Seattle
(WA) Public Library did with their "College Admissions and Scholarships"
program: http://tinyurl.com/osy6m7.

If you are fortunate enough to sponsor author visits, be sure to capture
their talks on podcasts, and post them on all possible online venues that
are linked to the library. Partner with school library media specialists to

promote the combination of reading the author's works as well as listening to the podcasts.

VIRTUAL READER'S ADVISORY

Introduce your regular teens to social networking sites for readers, where they can post books enjoyed, comment on others' reviews, and learn about exciting new titles to explore. readers' rants (http://readersrants. blogspot.com) and Goodreads (http://www.goodreads.com) are popular. Join Goodreads yourself to maintain personal booklists while at the same time befriending willing teen patrons to observe what they are into. When you see them in person, mention that you saw them on Goodreads and, hopefully, have an impromptu book discussion.

Explore Neal Wyatt's inspiring *Library Journal* article on the concept of Reading Maps, described as "web-based visual journeys through books that chart the myriad associations and themes of a title via other books, pictures, music, links to web sites, and additional material" (Wyatt, 2006). Have a group of teens agree on a book that would make an ideal reading map and collaborate on its design. What are appropriate read-alikes? Link them to your library's catalog as well as to Goodreads or LibraryThing. Ask them to imagine a soundtrack for the book—what songs would its characters have on their MP3 players? Link to associated YouTube videos. What fine art or modern photos reflect the book? Search for examples on Flickr, or have the teens spend time on their own photo or video shoot. Could they secure an interview with the author to either create a podcast or post a live chat? Perhaps the author could even meet them in Second Life, and they could subsequently share the transcript on the library's Web site. Host a contest in which different groups create Reading Maps for staff to evaluate and award prizes. This would be an ideal creative summer program.

WIKIS

Get teens to work together on the creation of your wiki. What should be included? Exciting new movie trailers, book links, programming information? The Sewickley (PA) Public Library has a nice "Sewiki"—with a link asking teens to friend their MySpace page. (http://sewickleylibraryteens. pbwiki.com).Try naming your wiki something like "My Favorite Books," and ask the teen creators to submit author biographies or comments and book descriptions as initial content. As users gradually get on board, they can edit and add to the content: read-alikes and links to author sites. Ask local high school English teachers to promote the public library's wiki in class. Show them the Internet Public Library's Teen Poetry Wiki (http://www.ipl.org/div/teenpoet), where members can freely express themselves and respect others' work and responses. Link your Web site to topical wikis so that teens can be direct participants on a special interest: World of Warcraft (http://www.wowwiki.com/Main_Page) and Runescape (http://runescape.wikia.com/wiki/RuneScape_Wiki).

As more tweens and teens seek technology for their communal entertainment, as school standards require the use of technology by 21st-century learners, and as college freshman are increasingly expected to have these skills down pat for class projects, libraries can help by offering the means to make it all relevant and fun. As of this writing, the combination of social networking with teen library programming is really in its infancy. Imagine the possibilities just months from now as more librarians realize that the way to reach their young adult patrons is through what is swiftly becoming their preferred method of communication and socialization. What is next? 3D environments are gaining ground as applied to online learning and even classroom instruction. How can the public library support this technology? How will kids be using the amazing graphics and animations that are impending as the Internet evolves into "Web 3.0"? As younger people rely more on handheld devices to organize and entertain them, what applications will public libraries develop to establish their relevancy in this realm? Please find my challenge at the end of chapter 10, in which I ask readers to collaborate and share technology-based ideas, ask one another for advice and practical help, and expand on the programming ideas here that are just the tip of the iceberg.

WORKS CITED

Wyatt, Neal. 2006. "LJ Series 'Redefining RA': Reading Maps Remake RA." *Library Journal*, November 1. http://www.libraryjournal.com/article/CA6383011.html (accessed May 23, 2009).

7

◇ ◇ ◇

HOMEWORK HELP WIDGETS: A SCHOOL–LIBRARY PARTNERSHIP

Andrew Wilson

In the spring of 2007, the three New York City public library systems, Brooklyn Public Library, the New York Public Library, and Queens Library, began searching for ways to boost student usage of their online homework help resources. In 2005 the libraries cooperatively launched a homework help Web site, http://homeworkNYC.org. The site featured library databases, librarian-created research guides, online textbooks, live tutoring, and Ask-A-Librarian services. Despite being named an Official Honoree of the 2006 Webby Awards and garnering lots of praise from local educators, the site struggled to find a wide (and constant) audience among students. In October 2007 the libraries received a collaborative planning grant from the Institute of Museum and Library Sciences for the project Engaging Students, Parents and Educators in the Creation of an Online Homework Help Resource.

The libraries then organized a series of focus groups with tween and teenage students about their online homework habits. Under the facilitation of Linda Braun of LEO: Librarians and Educators Online, the students soon made it clear that most of them were unlikely to use content from a library Web site for their homework, no matter what resources were offered. Student Internet usage tended to focus on search engine results

(Google) and social networking sites (MySpace). Only if a teacher assigned a specific Web site for homework would teens be inclined to try something new.

The libraries decided that if new students could not be brought to their online resources, then perhaps libraries needed to start bringing resources to students' online environments. The chosen method: Use the social networking sites students were already using. The easiest way to get content onto these sites is through a widget. Widgets are small pieces of programming code that can be easily added to a social networking homepage. They allow users to access applications and information from other sites without leaving their own homepages. Most social networkers are already familiar with widgets as recreational or communication tools. Frequently, the widgets play music and provide games, instant messaging, or e-mail on a social networking homepage.

There are many possibilities for library widgets; and in a second round of focus groups, students offered many suggestions for potential functions. A live tutoring or Ask-A-Librarian widget could allow students to get immediate responses to homework questions on their homepage. A database widget might allow students to search library databases as easily as they do search engines. Widgets could also be constructed to store user's patron information and automate the login process for the library databases. And a catalog widget could allow students to search library catalogs and reserve books.

The first widget, currently under development by the libraries, is a "bookshelf widget." The concept resembles the widgets from Goodreads, LibraryThing, or Shelfari, but it is targeted to local students and has some potential new capabilities. Students will be able to display the books they read on a virtual bookshelf located on their social networking homepages, blogs, Web pages, and so on. To interest students who are not avid readers, the widget will also display the videos they watch and the video games they play. Each time a student adds a new book, video, or game, the widget can send out notifications to their chosen "friends." Students can post reviews of their materials and comment on what others are reading or viewing. This makes the widget another social tool that the teens can use. Focus-group teens said the social aspect is the key to its widespread acceptance by students.

Through the bookshelf widgets, students can form multiple "book clubs" (groups of friends). A student might join a teen group at her local library and share a shelf of books with fellow group members as well as her local librarian. Or a student might join a citywide summer reading club and share a shelf of the books he reads in order to win prizes. Or a teacher could set up a classroom club and ask students to display and review books from a school reading list on another shelf.

The widgets will link book covers to library catalog records, enabling viewers to locate and reserve the books at their local libraries. The widget is being designed to work among multiple library systems so that users in one system can add friends in areas served by other systems while each one's widget remains linked to its own local system (if both library systems are registered in the network). Teens also stressed that the appearance of the widgets is very important. The bookshelf widgets will have customizable graphics.

Most of the usage is expected to come from students, who can share their shelves with friends who have similar interests. They can set up separate shelves for different genres such as manga or horror videos. They can create shelves for books they have recently read or a shelf of their top 10 favorite video games. Although the project is aimed at a student population, it is also expected that adults will find the widgets appealing. The NYC libraries are aiming to develop future widgets as open source projects so that they can be easily adopted and adapted by other libraries without cost.

The use of social networks for the delivery of academic content is a new and relatively untested concept. Understandably, there has been some reluctance on the part of schools to engage students through social networks. High-profile news stories about abuse of the networks have created a climate of added caution. Yet that is where students currently are. If libraries are going to make contact with them, libraries must be in those networks as well.

Currently, NYC schools filter out the social networking sites from their own computers. There may also be a lack of technical knowledge among educators about what a widget is and how it can be used in the curriculum. To overcome these obstacles, the NYC libraries are interested in developing widgets that will also work in places other than the social networks—iGoogle, desktops, blogs, and individual Web sites. This would enable teachers to work within a site of their own choosing and let students set up widgets outside of the social networks. At the same time, students would have the ability to pull their teachers' content into their own widgets on the social networks if they choose to.

In September 2008, the NYC public libraries received a National Leadership Grant from Institute of Museum and Library Sciences for the project Homework NYC Widgets: A Decentralized Approach to Homework Help by Public Libraries, to implement the development and promotion of new homework help widgets. A major portion of the grant is designated for outreach in the schools and within the public libraries themselves. The libraries plan to introduce the concept of homework widgets to students, teachers, and parents through grassroots outreach, through library staff training, and through their Web sites. Once there is a core group of widget users, it is assumed the social networks will virally promote the widgets. Friends will see them on peers' pages and add them to their own, where they will be picked up by new sets of friends. The great potential is that libraries will be able to make their resources available to the many students who do not currently visit our Web sites or physical buildings or get introduced to the homework widgets in their schools.

8

◇ ◇ ◇

FRIENDING YOUR COLLEAGUES: BEING PROFESSIONAL WITH WEB-BASED SOCIAL NETWORKING

Linda W. Braun

> Not that long ago, I needed some advice on the book business and thought to ask my friend Buzz Bissinger, the author of *Friday Night Lights* and *A Prayer for the City.* The only sticking point was, we'd never met.
> —David Carr, *Hey Friend, Do I Know You?*

What I like about that opening quote is what it says about uses of social networking, not to mention the way concepts such as friendship have been redefined. The tools and technologies now available within a Web environment give users the chance to talk to a vast, widely dispersed universe of people about topics of mutual interest. Friending the author of *Friday Night Lights* on Facebook and then communicating with him about his craft is the kind of professional opportunity that previously would not have been easy, but with the advent of Web-based social networking, it can happen with the click of a button, as long as the other person is willing and able.

There's been a lot of media attention about the ways in which social networking might be harmful to teens. And, as a result, many librarians have been prohibited from implementing social networking programs and services for and with teens. Nonetheless, it is important not to let the negative press limit the ways you can use social networking in your own professional life. The connections you can make via MySpace, Facebook, blogs, Twitter, and so on can greatly improve your chances of job success.

In June 2008 I wrote a blog post titled "Getting Involved = Being in the Know," for the blog of the Young Adult Library Services Association (YALSA). The post partly focused on how using social networking tools helps me keep up on topics related to teens and libraries and how these tools give me a chance to network with a far-flung group of colleagues. On the blog, I wrote,

> I see that keeping up with people virtually—via Twitter, Facebook, chat, IM, email, and so on—has been incredibly beneficial. I now know instantaneously via Twitter what YALSA colleagues are up to in their libraries and with teens. I discover immediately on Good Reads what YALSA colleagues are reading and what they think of each book read. Social networking technology has certainly helped us to stay in touch. (Braun, 2008)

There is no doubt in my mind that Web-based social networking tools help me succeed professionally.

In the next sections of this chapter, I discuss some of the skills required in teen librarianship and how specific social networking tools support those skills. (A list of social networking tools and resources is available at the end of the chapter.)

It is important to mention that I am making the assumption in this chapter that readers already have a basic understanding of what social networking is and have knowledge of how to use various social networking tools. For that reason, the chapter only minimally covers how specific social networking resources work.

Similarly, although a variety of social networking tools are mentioned within this chapter, the examples and tools discussed represent a jumping-off point and are just a fraction of what is available and possible.

UNDERSTANDING YOUTH DEVELOPMENT

The American Academy of Family Physicians describes adolescence as:

> The teenage years are a time of transition from childhood into adulthood. Teens often struggle with being dependent on their parents while having a strong desire to be independent. They may also feel overwhelmed by the emotional and physical changes they are going through. (Kelly, 2006)

Understanding this transition is a key aspect of teen service. For example, a librarian who understands why behavior can change radically within a short period of time—a teen might be very friendly one day and the next not want anything to do with you—can be useful in understanding how to approach teens on a daily basis and in grasping how to make connections without overstepping bounds.

Thus, one way to use social networks professionally is as a tool to help you keep up on the topic of youth development. Facebook, blogs, microblogs, and wikis, for example, are just some of the tools available in order to accomplish this:

- In general, Wikipedia is a good tool for getting started learning about topics of importance in teen librarianship. For example, if you are just starting to learn about street lit, graphic novels, anime, computer games, or youth development, you can look up the topic on Wikipedia to find out the basic issues and learn terminology related to the topic. Some of the leaders in the youth development field have contributed to the article on the topic of youth development—for example, the staff of the National Council for Families and Youth. And do not forget, if you are knowledgeable about the topic of youth development, that you can also contribute to the Wikipedia entry.

- Blogs are another good way to keep up with the topic of youth development and connect with others interested in it. You can read others' blogs, and through the comment feature available on most blogs, it is possible for you to add your thoughts to the discussion. When looking for blogs related to youth development, it is a good idea to expand your reading beyond organizations that are specifically devoted to youth development. Look for blogs on youth issues in general. For example, the YALSA blog, mentioned previously, includes postings that highlight the role libraries can play in youth development and discusses how librarians and other adults can help teens grow up successfully.

- When searching Google or other search engines for youth development–related blogs and organizations, use terms and phrases you uncovered in the Wikipedia entry on the topic in order to expand your search.

- Once you locate a blog you want to keep up with, remember that you can get a notification of what is newly posted using the blog's RSS feed. By using that technology, you do not have to remember to go back and check the blog regularly to see if something new has appeared. Instead, you will receive notification of what's new in youth development regularly in your RSS reader.

- Microblogs such as Twitter can also help keep you up-to-date on the topic of youth development. A search for the phrase "youth development" on Twitter leads to many posts that link to interesting and innovative programs that support youth development within a particular community. Within the search results you not only find what people are saying and implementing in the area of youth development, but you can also find organizations and people to follow on Twitter who can keep you up-to-date on the topic.

- Facebook fan pages offer you another way to connect with others interested in youth development. When an organization sets up a Facebook fan page, they can then make discussions, videos, photos, and more available to users. Facebook users can become a fan of the organization and connect with others interested in the topic—in this case, youth development.

- At the time this chapter was written, the search function for fan pages on Facebook was not as useful as most librarians might like it to be. For that reason, when looking for fan pages on the site, broaden your search and look for pages of specific organizations and agencies that you know work in the youth development field. For example, DoSomething.org sponsors a Facebook fan page. The easiest way to find that page is to search for "do something." Once you locate the Do Something fan page on Facebook, you'll find a good example of a resource to use to learn more about the field of youth development, as well as ideas on how you can integrate youth development ideas and practices more fully into your library's programs and services.

- Facebook, blogs, and wikis are also useful publishing platforms. Consider starting your own Facebook fan page, not just as a way to connect with teens, but also as a way to have discussions with organizations in your community about how best to support teens as they figure out how to be successful adults.

TEEN ADVOCACY

Speaking up for teens, and the value of teen library services, is an important aspect of teen librarianship. Social networking provides an array of opportunities for getting the word out about teens and libraries. Library blogs give you a perfect way to educate the community about the programs and services the library provides that support positive youth development. They are also a way to advocate for teens and the services the library provides to them. Actually, most social networking tools provide opportunities for teen advocacy. Consider the following examples:

- Web-based videos that show teens involved in positive activities can go a long way to helping people understand the benefits of supporting teens in the library and the community as a whole. Sites such as Animoto give you the opportunity to take images of teens involved in library programs and services and turn them into well-produced music videos. These videos can then be embedded in blogs and Web sites and can be uploaded to popular video sites such as YouTube, so that a variety of people can see teens demonstrating positive behaviors. Remember, if you use videos of teens in this way, you want to pay attention to the policies your library follows related to images of those under 18 displayed on the Web.

- Microblogs, such as Twitter, are another good way to advocate for teens. The short microblog format, usually a message of no more than 140 characters, lets you get the word out succinctly to a large group of people. Twitter users appreciate quick updates. If you create a Twitter account and then regularly post information about the constructive activities teens in your community are involved in, you are acting as an advocate for teens. Or if you post links on your Twitter account to information that focuses on the positive things that teens are doing in a community, you are advocating for teens.

Often people wonder if it is worth posting information in a variety of places (for example Facebook, Twitter, etc.) to advocate for teens—or, for that matter, for library programs and services. It usually *is* a good idea. By doing so, you will cast a wide net and be able to connect with a large group of people. It is also likely that you will have more of an opportunity to talk to members of the community whom you do not already know.

People also often wonder, how do I have the time to post across social networks? Posting to a variety of social networking sites does not have to be time-consuming. That's partly due to innovations in technology. Now there are ways to post to multiple sites all at once—for example, Ping.fm. Once you set up an account with Ping.fm, you can let the service know which social networking sites you want to post to. Then, whenever you write something on Ping and click the submit button, the content you created will post across the networks in which you participate.

Once you start getting the word out about teens via social networks, you may find that it is useful to have a single location for readers to read all that you are publishing. One way to do that is with FriendFeed, an aggregator of social network posts. Once you setup a FriendFeed account, you can publicize it as the one place to find out all you have to say about teens. This makes it easier for members of the community to be able to keep up on all of the ways you are advocating for teens.

Do not forget that advocating for teens includes helping teens speak up for themselves and providing opportunities for them to do that successfully. Audio and video technologies are a good way to help make this happen:

- Several libraries give teens the chance to talk about their lives via audio podcasts. One of the first libraries to use this format successfully was the Cheshire Public Library in Cheshire, Connecticut. Over the past several years, teens in the community have produced a monthly (except for summer months) audio podcast. These podcasts cover a wide variety of topics from books to music and from popular culture to technology. By giving teens the chance to produce these podcasts, teen librarian Sarah Kline Morgan demonstrates to the community a wide range of teen capabilities. That is strong teen advocacy.

- Ever since the launch of YouTube, video has been a powerful way for teens and librarians to advocate for each other. In the spring of 2008, members of a Multnomah County (OR) Library Teen Advisory Board produced a video titled *Books*, which is a take-off on the popular video that appeared on MySpace, *Shoes*. As with the podcasts produced by teens at the Cheshire Public Library, *Books* shows the Multnomah community, and other YouTube viewers, what teens are capable of, including their ability to use higher-order thinking skills such as parody and satire.

AWARENESS OF TEEN POPULAR CULTURE

You do not need to dress or act like teens or be interested in the same things in which teens are interested to be a successful teen librarian. However, it is important to have knowledge of current teen trends and what's hot in teen-related popular culture. This knowledge can help you build relevant collections as well as give you opportunities to talk with teens about what is important to them.

Web-based social networking tools have made keeping up with what's popular easier than ever before:

- YouTube does not simply allow teens to communicate their skills and ideas to their peers; it also gives you a chance to keep up with what is going on in popular culture, and teen popular culture in particular. Of course, not all of the popular videos on

YouTube are popular with all teens, so knowing what's hot on YouTube also gives you an opportunity to ask teens about their likes and dislikes, including the latest "viral" YouTube phenomenon. For example, the *Simon's Cat* series s that was popular in 2008.

- iGoogle, Netvibes, and Pageflakes are three start-page creation tools that make it easy to open up your Web browser and immediately see the latest information about a variety of teen-related topics. The widgets (also known as gadgets) that you can add to your start page include RSS feeds from blogs that focus on teen interests and popular culture, a list of most popular videos at YouTube, updates from those you follow on Twitter, and so on. With this start page you cannot miss what is going on in teen lives. Every time you open up your browser, you will be reminded of what's hot and what's not.

PROJECT MANAGEMENT

Although a librarian working with teens may not have entered the profession thinking of herself as a project manager, in reality, in order to be effective in the job, the ability to simultaneously manage a variety of projects and tasks is a key to success. Social networking has made it easier to be an effective project manager. Web-based tools that enable users to build calendars, create and collaborate on documents, or construct task lists are perfect for working on multiple projects at once and for collaborating on projects with colleagues and with teens. These tools also make it easier to take your project with you wherever you are. You do not need to carry around hard-copy task lists or calendars anymore. You can simply open up a Web browser, log in to an account, and get to work on your project. Here are some examples:

- Google provides a suite of tools to help you manage projects. For example, with Google Calendar you record the due dates for various pieces of a project. You might also include task lists in the comment fields so that those working on the project will be aware of the specifics of what is needed in order to get a particular item completed.
- Google calendars can be shared with others, and you can decide the level of access each person can have to a calendar. For example, you might have a calendar with dates for completing a variety of tasks on which the teen advisory board (TAB) is working. You can invite members of the TAB to the calendar and give them the

ability to add information to it. You can invite other teens, those not involved in the TAB, to the calendar as well, only as viewers, so that they can view dates but not update the calendar in any way.

- As with Google Calendar, Google Docs gives you the opportunity to give others access to your work. With Google Docs, you can create word processed documents, spreadsheets, and PowerPoint-style presentations. A document might be a task list for those working on a project with you. Each person on the project could add tasks to the list, update others on progress made, and so on. If the project you are working on requires a presentation of some sort, you can use the presentation feature of Google Docs to collaborate on the development of the presentation.

- Remember the Milk (RTM) is Web-based project management software that makes it easy to create, update, categorize, and collaborate on task lists. Once you set up an RTM account, you can start creating lists and then invite others to add their own tasks to the list or to just view a list.

- What makes RTM really powerful as a social networking project management tool is the ability to integrate RTM into other tools that you are using. For example, you can set up a list on RTM which will automatically be posted on your Google Calendar. Or you can have RTM send out text reminders of items that are due. RTM also works with Twitter, so anything in an RTM list you want to be made aware of can be sent as an update to your Twitter account.

- When people think of wikis, they usually think of Wikipedia and similar Web sites that provide information on a particular topic. But, wikis can also be used as project management tools. An example of this is the Web 2.0 planning wiki sponsored by the American Association of School Librarians (AASL). A group of AASL members surveyed the Web 2.0 landscape to determine how the organization could use the technologies available to serve members. As a part of the research process, a wiki was set up, where those working on the project could post information and let others know about plans, develop agendas, and discuss topics of interest.

COMMITMENT TO PROFESSIONAL DEVELOPMENT

There are a variety of ways to define professional development. Some people use the phrase as an umbrella when discussing organized classes and workshops developed to provide training on a topic to a group of people. Others use the phrase to describe any kind of learning that takes place and helps one keep up with and succeed in their workplace. Social networking makes it possible to meet the requirements of both definitions:

- VoiceThread is a presentation social networking tool that takes the concept of PowerPoint into an entirely different realm. With VoiceThread, it is possible to create narrated slide presentations. However, there is a twist: others who view the presentation can comment on it and ask questions. So, the presentation is not static; it is dynamic, and the content is revised and updated based on the feedback of viewers.

- An example of a use of VoiceThread is librarian Rebecca Mazur's demonstration of a clever tool, Awesome Highlighter, which allows users to emphasize text on Web sites. In her VoiceThread presentation, Mazur does a good job at demonstrating how Awesome Highlighter can be used successfully for professional development. Her overview of Awesome Highlighter is useful when learning about the tool. However, what makes this presentation even better is the fact that others have asked questions about Awesome Highlighter, and Rebecca and other users have answered. Anyone who views the presentation can learn from Rebecca and all of the others who have experience with the software.

- Learning from others is a key aspect of Web-based social networking, and another way you can learn within the social network environment is through movies and visual presentations that are embedded in Web sites, blogs, wikis, and so on. For example, tutorials are no longer available just in text format. In the social network world, you can now view a video tutorial for a piece of equipment or software. Often you can also post comments related to the tutorial and get answers from other viewers and users of the product.

- Similarly, many conference presenters are now making their presentations available for embedding on Web sites via social networking tools such as SlideShare. SlideShare enables users to upload presentations to the site and then add those presentations to a blog, wiki, Web page, and so on. SlideShare is searchable, so even if a presentation is not available outside of the SlideShare site, you can search for a topic of interest, locate a presentation on that topic, view the presentation, and discuss with others.

- There was a time when producing Web-based live video broadcasts was a costly and difficult proposition. Fortunately, that has changed, and now there are several different Web-based companies that make it possible for ordinary people to stream live video in order to hold classes and meetings. To take part in one of these broadcasts, all you need is a computer and high-speed Internet access.

- What moves these broadcasts into the social network realm is that during a presentation viewers can chat with the presenter and other participants. This makes it possible to ask questions during a presentation, even if you are not in the room, and to learn not only from the presenter but also from those who are participating in the live stream.

- More and more organizations that sponsor conferences, and conference presenters, are using this technology to reach those who cannot travel to the conference venue. For your own professional development, check out whether conference presentations you are interested in are going to be presented in this format. If so, you will be able to participate from the comfort of your own home or library. If the presentation is archived, you will be able to participate on your own schedule.

DON'T WAIT; START CONNECTION NOW

As I was writing this chapter, Fresno County (CA) Public Library librarians Connie Urquhart and Lisa Lindsay e-mailed me about a social networking experience they had had, which typifies what has been discussed here. Here's what happened:

Connie is a blogger for YALSA. She posted an entry on the blog about how the Great Stories program, a reading program sponsored by YALSA and ALA, made a difference in the lives of incarcerated teens in Fresno. As a part of the post, Connie mentioned how much the teens enjoyed reading Coe Booth's book *Tyrell*.

Lisa Lindsay, an avid Twitter user, is a friend of Coe Booth on Twitter. (They have not met face-to-face and know each other only via Twitter.) After reading Connie's post, Lisa sent a Twitter message that let Coe (and others) know about Connie's blog post. Coe read the Twitter message and wrote on Twitter about how happy she was to learn about the positive impact her book had on teens.

Then Lisa and Coe started a conversation via Twitter direct messages— these are Twitter messages that are private just between two people— about Coe visiting Lisa's library when she travels to California for some speaking engagements. The conversation progressed, and sure enough, it is very possible that Coe Booth will be visiting the Fresno County Library System.

The story of Connie, Lisa, and Coe highlights how social networking provides teen librarians with expanded opportunities for improving library services and connecting professionally with people of interest to teens and to the librarians that serve them. If Lisa had not sent the original Twitter message, teens in Fresno might have missed an opportunity to get to hear their favorite author, in person.

Do not be afraid to use the new technologies available. They will make it easier for you to be better at your job: providing excellent service to, and strong advocacy for, teens.

SOCIAL NETWORKING RESOURCES FOR THE PROFESSIONAL TEEN LIBRARIAN
Social Networking Tools

The following list of social networking resources were mentioned in this chapter as tools to use in order to enhance your skills as a teen librarian.

Animoto
http://www.animoto.com

Facebook
http://www.facebook.com

FriendFeed
http://www.friendfeed.com

Google Calendar
http://calendar.google.com

Google Docs
http://docs.google.com

iGoogle
http://igoogle.com

MySpace
http://www.myspace.com

Netvibes
http://www.netvibes.com

Pageflakes
http://www.pageflakes.com

Ping.fm
http://www.ping.fm

Remember the Milk
http://www.rememberthemilk.com

SlideShare
http://www.slideshare.com

Twitter
http://www.twitter.com

Twitter Search
http://search.twitter.com

Ustream
http://www.ustream.tv

Wikipedia
http://www.wikipedia.com

YouTube
http://www.youtube.com

Examples of Social Networking as a Professional Tool

AASL Web 2.0 Wiki
http://aasl20taskforce.wikispaces.com

Awesome Highlighter on VoiceThread
http://ed.voicethread.com/share/162112

Books
http://www.youtube.com/watch?v=vLmtkD1kiK0

Cheshire Public Library Teen Podcasts
http://www.cheshirelib.org/teens/cplpodcast.htm

Coe Booth on Twitter

http://www.twitter.com/coebooth

Connie Urquhart on Twitter

http://www.twitter.com/connieurq

DoSomething.org Facebook Fan Page

http://www.facebook.com/pages/Do-Something/7630216751

Lisa Lindsay on Twitter

http://www.twitter.com/trmite

Simon's Cat

http://www.youtube.com/user/simonscat?blend=1&ob=4

YALSA Blog

http://yalsa.ala.org/blog

WORKS CITED

Braun, Linda. 2008. *Getting Involved = Being in the Know.* June 24. http://yalsa.ala. org/blog/2008/06/24/getting-involved (accessed May 23, 2009).

Kelly, Robert B., ed. 2006. *Understanding Your Teenager's Emotional Health.* November. http://familydoctor.org/online/famdocen/home/children/parents/ parents-teens/590.html (accessed May 23, 2009).

9

◇ ◇ ◇

A NATIONAL VIEW:
SURVEY—AND A CHALLENGE

Robyn M. Lupa

In the Fall of 2007 I used Zoomerang to initiate a survey of librarians who work with teens on the topic of social networking. I posted it on the PUBLIB, PUBYAC, and the yalsa-bk e-mail lists, and 118 respondents from around the country allowed me to gain an interesting perspective on what is happening in public libraries. I would like to thank those respondents for their time, observations, and honesty and for motivation for the direction of this book.

Overwhelmingly, the respondents observed their teen patrons using library computers for social networking (91%), with gaming and visiting virtual worlds as a runner-up (78%). MySpace was, at the time, the most popular site accessed, with 86 percent of the respondents listing it at the top.

When asked what they felt inspired the popularity of social networking sites among teens, answers reflected what you have been reading in this book: a chance to show off individual personalities and "coolness"—both to peers and to complete strangers; a way to have instant access to and keep in touch with friends; a desire to post pictures and receive instant feedback and the appealing creativity inherent in the technology; the ability to be bold, expressive, and unrestrained in their communication; and the simplicity of social networking—proper spelling and grammar are not required! Other comments included these quotes from respondents:

Just a way to connect. A little bit of a way to talk about yourself ("We're going to my grandma's...ugh!") and find out what your friends are up to in short little bursts without it having to be a big long conversation.

Ability to "check out" others without being noticed. Gathering "friends" from around the country and world. Competition to get the most "friends."

Because it's a form of instant communication—this age group is totally into communicating electronically vs. personally (i.e., text-messaging over cell phones).

No face to face meeting, freedom to speak your mind, excitement of having "no limit."

Social networking sites allow the teen to create their own place free of adults, where they can be whatever they want. I think the appeal is that they can be dramatic/epic, individual, independent, and still hang out with friends. I also consider it the phone or diner "chill" spot of previous generations. Only the format has changed.

Sensory Overload!!! Pictures, music, popularity voting through "friending" and the easy ability to personalize their "space."

In middle school and high school, clique relationships and popularity and gossip and friendship and dating are really important. Social networking sites simply allow teens to take those things online.

They are relatively easy to set up and use, and provide a commonality among groups of friends...one place where everyone can meet up.

The ability to connect with others on a superficial level. By this I mean that they are at once revealing a lot about themselves (e.g., name, birthdate, tastes in music, etc.) and at the same time nothing at all. Social networking sites also allow for the self promotion and visibility that have become the norm in our culture.

It allows teens to socialize even more than they normally would. Instead of only being able to socialize with certain friends during certain times (school, scheduled visits, etc.) they can socialize virtually nonstop 24 hours a day. I think there's a bit of a contest aspect too—I have more friends than you, whose friends are cooler, my pictures are cooler, my website is cooler. I think it's also a great method of self-expression for teens. They want to display their personality without being too obvious. They can do that on a social networking website by the background they choose, the funky little tools, the background music, and all the little blurbs they can put in about themselves. It's about making themselves seem as neat and cool as possible.

They are more private than the telephone. No one can listen in. They can socialize with multiple people. They don't have to go anywhere to meet people. They can be whoever they want to be because the people online don't see them.

I think what our patrons like about MySpace is that it allows them to reinvent themselves (or perhaps to define who they are) online, and then share that with their friends. They might not have a lot of money or a hot girlfriend, but they can certainly make that part of their profile.

Teens can build networks of new friends while keeping in touch with old friends. The communities served by the libraries I manage include military personnel. Many teens from military families use MySpace to keep in touch with friends from the cities and towns where they used to live.

It is a way for them to connect with each other, share information, and just generally socialize. It strikes me as being a way to relax and kick back after a long day of sitting in desks and being talked at by teachers. It's a place where they can be themselves.

It's a way to connect with so many other people. For teens in this rural area, it has to be like a window to the "outside" world.

The ability to interact with the world, without truly engaging it, is enticing. Especially for teens who may be shy, anti-social, unpopular or just curious about a part of the world they do not participate in. This kind of voyeurism, in a sense of the word, allows them to see into, without real and physical consequence, their peers' lives, strangers' lives, and other parts of their own lives.

It provides for community, one of our basic human needs.

Sixty-one percent of these librarians who work with teens had a MySpace or Facebook page of their own. Most got onto the sites to see firsthand what the hype was all about. Beyond being curious about the technology, some joined for professional development, or so that they could respond to patron questions on how to change a page's background color, how to upload photos, and how to change passwords. Many remained, as a method of staying in touch with friends, family, and casual acquaintances and following musicians. Some were actually communicating with teen patrons via their MySpace page.

But 62 percent of their employers did not have a presence on MySpace or Facebook. They expressed frustrations with resistant administration or IT departments. Following are the words of some of the respondents:

> To this point our library system will not support branch-based social networking sites. I'm hoping they'll see the importance of this before too long.
>
> I wish my library would allow us to create a MySpace page for our teens.
>
> Totally not allowed (but I really want one)! MySpace is still viewed as a suspicious site filled with stalkers and porn by our library admin.
>
> Not only has my library not created a MySpace site, but it has blocked access to MySpace on account of the "disruptive" teens who used to visit the library to use it...sigh.

However, those 38 percent of respondents who had institutional sites encountered a variety of experiences with them. They wrote the following:

> Used to advertise upcoming programs, events and contests; post lists of books used in monthly HS Reader's Club; accept messages from teens to answer questions, do reader's advisory and other reference activity.
>
> We get a lot of teen friends on our MySpace, and use the site and the bulletins to post about events and news. I'm not sure how often it gets read, but we keep trying.
>
> I found that the teens I interact with the most are actually not on MySpace and have since found my personal Facebook account. Our library MySpace is not used much at all. I think because the teens prefer a personal connection with the librarian to the general MySpace page. I do use the MySpace for advertising programs and books, just to cover all the bases.
>
> I am solely in charge of updating/monitoring, and I access the site a couple times a week. Patrons (teens) seem glad to have that connection with me.
>
> We only recently started the MySpace page, so usage is low, but steadily increasing. It's very easy to update on a weekly basis, and it's self-contained. Everything I want to post can be seen on one page which is very nice. We only accept authors and organizations as friends at this time. We're hesitant to accept teens as friends because we can not control what is on their page, and it is too time

consuming to check each friend everyday to make sure that nothing offensive is posted.

We get a decent amount of traffic on our MySpace site. The staff thought the idea was creepy at first but it has turned out to be a great way to reach our most-difficult–to-connect-with patrons.

We use the MySpace page to send out announcements about upcoming events, to post pictures from past events, and to answer questions from our teen patrons (both library and personal questions).

I use it as a means of communicating with my teens. MySpace is blocked on our teen computers so they can't access it in the library. Most of my friends on MySpace are my high schoolers. My middle schoolers have Bebo.

Most of the teens that use the library have friended the library on MySpace as well. The page is updated regularly to include newly arrived books, CDs and movies, as well as publicize upcoming events.

When asked whether librarians had experienced issues surrounding the use of social networking sites by teens in the library, if they had been in a position to discuss concerns with parents and/or educators, and if their library had developed guidelines or restrictions on what teens may access, the responses varied. A number of libraries opted to block the use of MySpace and Facebook, denying teens access to them. Others had not encountered problems.

We filter our computers, we used to block MySpace but after convincing from our YA librarian we now give access. We haven't had any problems so far, but they do bully over IM.

We haven't had any problems, and haven't had any parents speak up about anything. I'm trying to get a workshop for parents started to introduce them to social networking, but it's going very slowly. We have not developed guidelines, but our public computers are filtered.

As a public school librarian, our web filter—Websense—censors out all links to social networks online. Students do not have the ability to send or receive email from any provider while on a school computer.

I have held workshops that discuss all of the above with teens and encourage parental discussion/knowledge of what their teens are doing on-line.

I haven't had to address parental concerns on this topic. We don't have restrictions for teens. We've offered programs for parents but get little response.

We've had some trainings with local police for both parents and teens, but they are not well attended. I do have ALA's bookmarks about internet safety in the YA area of the library.

No restrictions; kids have the same rights and freedoms as adults. It is the parents' job to monitor their children, not ours.

We don't restrict teens' access to social networking sites. We have had programs for teens and for parents about internet safety. We also have a lot of flyers and bookmarks. The teens seem VERY aware of the risks.

Yes. I talk with teens frequently about privacy concerns and revealing too much personal information. The library has invited speakers who have expertise in this subject area, but participation by teens in these sessions has been limited. The library has a computer use policy that addresses some of these issues but not specifically social networking.

There was a brief time when our library wanted to ban the use of MySpace. But we responded that that was sending a message to the teens that we don't want them there and I felt it was over-reactive. A few parents have complained about teens looking at racy MySpace pictures. We send the teens out to the adult section if that's the case. Social networking is a HUGE part of teens social lives!

Other than its rabid consumption of our very limited bandwidth, we have not first-hand experienced negativity due to social networking sites.

Some libraries did have problems, as indicated in these quotes from respondents:

Our library has blocked MySpace. We had a lot of issues with gang activity and X-rated photos being viewed, and also, teens could get rowdy when they gathered around the computers to go on MySpace.

I've had one instance of cyberbullying, and another teen helped with the technical options while I helped with the social/psychological impact. I have not had an opportunity to discuss the issue with other non-library adults. Our library requires teens under 17 to have filtered access, but other than that there are no restrictions placed on their access.

When asked if they had offered programming for teens that partners technology and reading—for example, online summer reading clubs, online book discussions, or MySpace groups dedicated to specific books or authors—a large number, 79 percent, of respondents had not done so (although many hoped they would soon). However, the 21 percent that did develop programming in that area were mostly using online book discussions or blogs with book reviews and book trailers or, in one case, creating video book-talks.

The next question asked whether librarians had hosted programming for teens that reflected their general interest in technology, such as video- or photo-sharing workshops, sessions on developing MySpace pages, or online gaming nights. A larger number, 52 percent, of the respondents were involved in that sort of programming. Aside from numerous gaming events, happenings that they described included the following:

> We have a Teen Tech Club which teaches teens about things they might not know about the Internet: wikis, open source, rss, html, invisible internet, etc.

> We have frequent video game programs (we have Wii and PS2 with several games each, including DDR, Guitar Hero, etc.). We're planning some video game tournaments, too. We've tried to start an online photography contest, but it got held up by the system and hasn't happened yet.

> MySpace program open to parents as well.

> We have had photo manipulation contests, etc. We also will be celebrating Teen Tech Week in 2008.

> I ran a workshop that taught blogging.

> We do many online gaming events from XBox 360 to PC gaming. We also offer classes on many things like podcasting, MySpace improvement, Flickr, and many others.

> We have Nintendo Wii gaming and will be hosting our first film festival in the spring. We also regularly let our teens use our digital cameras and camcorders to create their own works of art.

> We had a Mod My Profile event in which I helped teens alter their MySpace profiles—it included a little html and css.

> Classes in web publishing and blogging using Google's free tools.

> We did a program…Pimp the Librarian's MySpace. We also host video gaming tournaments weekly.

> Our system as a whole recently held a video contest to promote our Live Homework Help service. Just in the last month or so, we

developed a MySpace page for the library and are letting teens help update it. Finally, I have had the occasional online gaming night. In my particular branch I can't have World of Warcraft nights or anything involving installation of software on the computers. The teens are perfectly happy with extra time on Runescape or MySpace, though.

We are going to hold a program in February on creating your own video and uploading it to sites like YouTube.

We are part of the Project Next Generation Grant group, which helps them explore new technology.

This winter we are offering a Teen and Tween Computer Club where teens will be able to create their own animations and games using Scratch—free software offered by MIT. We are also holding a Teen Movie Festival where teens will learn about making movies, will create their own, and will be awarded prizes.

I-tunes creation workshop.

Potential summer reading programming is based on the MySpace theme.

Game Design Studio using the program Scratch; improving your MySpace page; Gaming (DDR, Guitar Hero, Wii); Runescape Roundtable; after-school tutoring, technology and gaming program called ttyl.

The library holds a monthly Teen Night and those present may have access to all public computers (not just the ones designated for teens). They may use them for gaming or social networking.

The final question asked if librarians had partnered with educational institutions on technology-based instruction or technology-oriented programming for teens. Sadly, 87 percent had not participated in this. Those who had were actively visiting schools to perform database and catalog demonstrations. Other ideas were offered by the respondents:

I've partnered with the local community college to offer computer instruction to the public at my library. I am working with them to develop some basic classes on HTML and whatnot to be used on MySpace.

We are partnering with a local museum to have our teens use digital cameras and camcorders to record their thoughts and opinions of the galleries.

I'm just beginning a tutoring program with our local high school in the library that will hopefully incorporate technology based learning.

New course to start in new year focusing on technology/career advice for teens in partnership with adult education.

Ongoing Game Design Studio and Gaming programs are part of a 21st Century After School Success grant w/our local school district. The program development is ours, but the school provides transportation and promotion of the program; funding is federal.

There is a lot being done by public libraries in an effort to advocate, educate, and dedicate technology to teens in the realm of social networking. The survey reveals that many libraries have not yet embraced the movement or are just starting out. I hope this book, with examples from leaders in the field, educators and testimony from a teen, proves how vital it is for public libraries who work with teens to commit themselves to Web 2.0 and how it has changed the way teens learn, form their identities, and express and entertain themselves.

Now that we have a solid foundation as to what social networking is all about, I challenge everyone—including you!—to jump on board with me. I have established a wiki at http://morethanmyspace.wetpaint.com/. Let's explore this technology by talking about what we are doing in our own institutions. Whether you are observing teens in action with Web 2.0, planning programs on that topic, or having a conversation with teens on your Facebook page—all contributions to the discussion are welcome. Join me at this site for ideas, resources, research, easy access to all links that are included in this book, and—most important—a healthy dialogue among librarians who are out there using the technological tools.

APPENDIX: TOP 20 SOCIAL NETWORKING SITES

Dave Moyer

Dave Moyer, 16 years old at the time of this book's publication, was asked to submit his top 20 list of social networking sites for this publication. Below is that list, in no order of preference.

NETWORK	DESCRIPTION	URL
Ping.fm	Not exactly a network, but the definitively most useful tool for just about every social networking site. Ping.fm gives you the ability to post to multiple Web sites at once. You can group sites together yourself or just use Ping.fm's built-in categories like Micbro.	http://ping.fm
Twitter	The original microblogging site. Known for its scaling problems and humorous error messages. Users can post messages up to 140 characters in length and follow what others are posting.	http://twitter.com

(*continued*)

NETWORK	DESCRIPTION	URL
Plurk	Similar to Twitter, Plurk is a microblogging service with a more graphical interface. Users view messages of those they "follow" in a timeline-style interface and can add messages based on prefixes like *username* "is," "was," "will," "likes," "wants," or the useful ":".	http://www.plurk.com
Delicious	Delicious (formerly del.icio.us) is the classic link-sharing site. Users bookmark Web sites they want to share with other users, tagging them with topics or other users that the link may be "for." Links added appear in their profile or perhaps in the popular links box on the Delicious homepage.	http://delicious.com
FriendFeed	FriendFeed allows users to roll their entire online presence into one feed, where their friends can follow along with everything they do. From Plurk posts to Facebook status updates—all appear in a user's FriendFeed. The service also gives users the ability to post short messages just to their FriendFeed.	http://friendfeed.com
Facebook	One of the most popular "classic" social networking sites. Users create a profile and network with other members. Unique to Facebook are its applications, including games, quizzes, and more.	http://facebook.com
LinkedIn	LinkedIn is the original business social networking site. Users create a resume-style profile and add "connections" based on real-world business relationships. The site also includes a job directory.	http://www.linkedin.com
YouTube	Everyone knows YouTube these days. The classic video-sharing site allows users to upload and comment on videos and befriend other users. It also includes functionality for users to subscribe to another's channel, receiving updates on when that user uploads a new video.	http://www.youtube.com
Ustream	Ustream is a live video site. Users create "shows" where they can broadcast live video right from their computer. Ustream	http://ustream.tv

(continued)

NETWORK	DESCRIPTION	URL
	includes functionality to record videos, has a live chat room for each show, and gives users the ability to "follow" other users to see when they are live.	
Flickr	Flickr is the original photo-sharing site. Users can upload photos to their account, adding to specific sets of pictures. Different photos can be either public or private (only contacts can view them) at the user's discretion. Owned by Yahoo!	http://www.flickr.com
Digg	Digg is a link-popularity Web site. Users submit links, which can then be "dug" or "buried." The most "dug" stories appear on the Digg homepage, sending large amounts of traffic to that specific Web site.	http://digg.com
Brightkite	Brightkite is the first "location-based" social network. Users can check in at different locations by either their cell phone or their browser, chat with other users in their location, and post photos and messages about where they are. (And, of course, you can add friends.)	http://brightkite.com
Stickam	Similar to Ustream and a bit older in age, Stickam allows users to create a single live video stream and includes a chat room and recorded video functionality. Stickam also allows users to become "friends" with others.	http://www.stickam.com
Identi.ca	Another "Twitter-killer" hopeful, Identi.ca is simply your basic blogging service. What makes it unique is the fact that it has released its source code to give users the ability to create their own microblogging sites.	http://identi.ca/
MySpace	Possibly the engines behind the rocket of social networking. Though there were Web sites before it, MySpace took off like no other. Users add friends, create their profile, send messages, chat, comment, and even browse music and videos.	http://www.myspace.com

(continued)

NETWORK	DESCRIPTION	URL
Stumble Upon	StumbleUpon adds a "Stumble" button to users' browsers, sending them to a random Web site based on their interests. Users can recommend a link or give it a "thumbs-down." Recommendations appear on their profile for their friends and other users to enjoy.	http://www. stumbleupon. com
Last.fm	Last.fm allows users to create their own "radio station," picking artists and songs they like and listening to them online. The site, of course, allows you to add friends and see what music they're listening to. Last.fm recommends songs that you may like and offers methods to purchase albums and tracks.	http://www. last.fm
Pownce	Pownce is one of the most popular microblogging sites. Like Twitter, you can post short messages to the service, which appear in a list format. Pownce also allows users to post photos and videos in their messages.	http://pownce. com/
Jaiku	Jaiku, is similar to Twitter and Pownce. It is a microblogging service, popular for its ability to post to other sites such as Twitter.	http://jaiku. com
Viddler	Viddler is very similar to most video-sharing sites like YouTube. What sets it apart, however, is the ability to annotate and comment on videos as you are watching them and to see what other users have commented as the video plays. Comments pop up like thought bubbles at the bottom of the player.	http://www. viddler.com

GLOSSARY OF TERMS

Application—an application program is designed to perform a function for a computer user. Examples include word processors, library databases, and search engines.

Avatar—in 3D or virtual reality environments such as Second Life and in some chat forums on the Web, your avatar is the visual "handle" or graphical appearance that you choose to represent yourself.

Blog—a shortened term for "Web log," this is a collaborative threaded discussion in an online forum. Blogs are typically owned by one person who posts an article or other piece of writing. Visitors are allowed to view the posting and leave comments that create a thread or Web log of the written dialog.

Chat—also know as chat rooms, these areas allow Internet users to send a quick instant message and hold a typewritten conversation with another Internet user. There is a logged activity of the chat history.

Cyberculture—the culture that has emerged from using the Internet for communication through e-mail, chat, blogs, wikis, and social networking applications.

Cyberspace—a domain characterized by the use of electronic devices and electronic media; sometimes used synonymously with the terms "World Wide Web" or the "Internet."

Digital divide—the gap between people who do and do not have adequate access to computers and the Internet and—consequently—access to information and electronic methods of communication.

Digital media—an electronic version that represents a physical form of communication, such as an eBook delivered through a library database on the Internet.

Digital publics—areas within the cyberculture where people hang out online to replace hanging out in brick-and-mortar locations such as the shopping mall.

Friend—a person or an avatar added to one's social network in an online digital public.

Geo-caching—a treasure hunting game played outdoors in which participants use a GPS or another navigation receiver to hide and seek containers (caches) containing log books and minor treasure anywhere in the world.

Instant message—a real-time chat exchange sent through the Internet that is not archived as a Web log.

Microblog—a form of blogging where you can write a short text update, send a link to a Web page such as Facebook, or share photo and audio clips. The messages can be submitted by text messaging from a cell phone, by e-mail, or by instant messaging.

Mobile application—a program that is designed to perform a function for a mobile (cellular or cell) phone user or another application. Examples include text messaging or Internet browsers used on the phone's interface.

Moblogging—the act of connecting to a blog using a text message or mobile application.

Photo sharing—posting or transferring digital photos online in order to share them with others.

Podcast—audio recordings, generally as MP3 files, distributed for download to digital music or multimedia players. A podcast is usually a series such as a news report or an author lecture program that people subscribe to and receive on a regular basis.

Primary source—an original and authoritative media or documentation pertaining to an event or subject of inquiry that serves as a firsthand or eyewitness account of an event or subject.

Profile—available information about an Internet user or the person behind an avatar, such as name, birthday, profession, or even hobbies and interests.

RSS—a channel on the World Wide Web known as a "feed" that is used to publish works that are frequently updated, such as blog entries, news headlines, and audio and video files.

Social bookmarking—Internet applications that allow people to store, categorize, annotate, and share their favorite Web sites or files. Twine, Delicious, and StumbleUpon are examples.

Tag—a generic term for a decipher or descriptor that is used to mark up any form of digital media, making it easier to search and locate in a database.

Tag cloud—a list of all tags that are used within a single blog or Web page. This provides a visual representation of popular topics.

Text messaging—a mobile application that allows people to send each other small messages via their cell phone.

21st-century learning—an educational approach that includes emerging technologies to address the "whole child." Its curriculum includes tackling complex problems, teamwork, using technology for communication, and an appreciation and awareness of global issues.

Virtual reality—an artificial environment that is created and presented to people in such a way that they suspend belief and accept it as a real environment. Second Life is an example of this type of artificial environment.

Vlog—video files used as a Web log.

Web 2.0—a term coined by O'Reilly Media mogul Tim O'Reilly and used to define the new age of digital media applications used on the Internet such as Flickr, MySpace, Second Life, blogs, wikis, and RSS feeds.

Widget—an element of a graphical user interface on a computer or mobile device that displays information or provides a specific way for a user to interact with the application program. Widgets include icons, pull-down menus, buttons, selection boxes, progress indicators, on-off checkmarks, scroll bars, windows, forms, and many other devices for displaying information and for inviting, accepting, and responding to user actions.

Wiki—originally comes from the Hawaiian word "wikiwiki," or "fast." A wiki is a server application program that allows people to collaborate in the formation of digital media content over the Internet for a term, a concept, or even a project.

FURTHER READING

Armstrong, M., and J. Arrowsmith. 2008. *The Power Libraries Program*. Colorado Department of Education, September 29. http://www.cde.state.co.us/cdelib/powerlib/goals.htm (accessed May 23, 2009).

Armstrong, S., and D. Warlick. 2004. "The new literacy." *Tech & Learning*. http://www.techlearning.com/article/2806 (accessed May 23, 2009).

Berlin, L. (2009). "Software that guards virtual playgrounds." *The New York Times*. April 18. http://tinyurl.com/ngvu35 (accessed June 2, 2009).

boyd, d. 2008. *Apophenia: Making Connections Where None Previously Existed*. http://www.zephoria.org/thoughts (accessed May 23, 2009).

Casey, M. E., and L. C. Savastinuk. 2007. *Library 2.0: A Guide to Participatory Library Service*. Medford, NJ: Information Today, Inc.

Common Sense Media. 2006. *Internet Survival Guide for Parents*. http://www.commonsense.com/internet-safety-guide (accessed May 23, 2009).

Conversants. (2009). *Web 2.0 Tutorials*. http://conversants.ning.com/page/web-20-tutorials (accessed June 2, 2009).

Council on 21st Century Learning. 2008. *Education Change*. http://www.c21l.org/educationchange.html (accessed May 23, 2009).

Courtney, N. 2007. *Library 2.0 and Beyond: Innovative Technologies and Tomorrow's User*. Westport, CT: Libraries Unlimited.

Crawford, W. 2007. *Public Library Blogs: 252 Examples*. Mountain View, CA: Cities & Insights.

Engard, N. 2008. *What I Learned Today*. http://www.web2learning.net (accessed May 23, 2009).

Farkas, M. 2008. *Library Success: A Best Practices Wiki.* http://www.libsuccess.org/
index.php?title=Main_Page (accessed May 23, 2009).

Farkas, M. 2008. "What Friends Are For: Capitalizing on Your Online Rolodex."
American Libraries 39 (1/2): 36.

Hargardon, S. 2007. "A little help from my friends: Classroom 2.0 educators
share their experiences." *School Library Journal,* October 1. http://www.
schoollibraryjournal.com/article/CA6484336.html (accessed May 23, 2009).

Harris, F. J. 2005. *I Found It on the Internet: Coming of Age Online.* Chicago: American
Library Association.

Hill, C. 2008. *Libraries Build Communities.* http://librariesbuildcommunities.org
(accessed May 23, 2009).

Kelsey, C. M. 2007. *Generation MySpace: Helping Your Teen Survive Online Adolescence.* New York: Marlowe & Company.

Kroski, E. 2008. "Widgets to the Rescue." *School Library Journal,* February 1. http://
www.schoollibraryjournal.com/article/CA6527346.html (accessed May 23,
2009).

Melton, B., and S. Shankle. 2007. *What in the World Are Your Kids Doing Online? How
to Understand the Electronic World Your Children Live In.* New York: Broadway
Books.

Murphy, J. and H. Moulaison. (2009). *Social Networking Literacy Competencies
for Librarians: Exploring Considerations and Engaging Participation.* http://
www.resourceshelf.com/2009/05/22/paper-social-networking-literacy-
competencies-for-librarians-exploring-considerations-and-engaging-
participation (accessed June 2, 2009).

Oldenburg, R. 2001. *Celebrating the Third Place: Inspiring Stories about the "Great Good
Places" at the Heart of Our Communities.* New York: Marlowe & Company.

Owyang, J. (2009). "The future of the social web: In five eras." April 27. http://
www.web-strategist.com/blog/2009/04/27/future-of-the-social-web
(accessed June 2, 2009).

Palfrey, J. 2008. *Born Digital: Understanding the First Generation of Digital Natives.*
New York: Basic Books.

Prensky, M. 2005. "Adopt and adapt: Shaping tech for the classroom." *Edutopia,*
December. http://www.edutopia.org/adopt-and-adapt (accessed May 23,
2009).

Rethlefsen, M. L. 2007. "Tags help make libraries Del.icio.us." *Library Journal,*
September 19. http://www.libraryjournal.com/article/CA6476403.html
(accessed May 23, 2009).

Rheingold, H. 2000. *The Virtual Community: Homesteading on the Electronic Frontier.*
Cambridge, MA: MIT Press.

Rheingold, H. 2002. *Smart Mobs: The Next Social Revolution.* Cambridge, MA: Per-
seus Publishing.

Richardson, W. 2008. *Weblogg-ed.* http://weblogg-ed.com (accessed May 23,
2009).

Rigby, B. 2008. *Mobilizing Generation 2.0: A Practical Guide to Using Web 2.0 Technologies to Recruit, Organize, and Engage Youth.* San Francisco: Jossey-Bass.

Rosen, L. D. 2007. *Me, Myspace and I: Parenting the Net Generation.* New York: Pal-
grave Macmillan.

Salaway, G., J. B. Caruso, and M. R. Nelson. 2008. *The ECAR Study of Undergraduate Students and Information Technology, 2008.* October 21. http://connect. educause.edu/Library/ECAR/TheECARStudyofUndergradua/47485 (accessed May 23, 2009).

Sauers, M. P. 2006. *Blogging and RSS: A Librarian's Guide.* Medford, NJ: Information Today.

Stephens, M. 2006. *Web 2.0 and libraries: Best practices for social software.* Chicago: American Library Association TechSource.

Stephens, M. 2008. *Tame the Web.* http://www.tametheweb.com (accessed May 23, 2009).

Tapscot, D. 1998. *Growing Up Digital: The Rise of the Net Generation.* New York: McGraw-Hill.

Thompson, C. 2008. "Brave new world of digital intimacy." *New York Times,* September 7. http://www.nytimes.com/2008/09/07/magazine/07awareness-t.html (accessed May 23, 2009).

Valenza, J. 2008. *Springfield Township High School Virtual Library.* http://www.sdst. org/shs/library (accessed May 23, 2009).

Valenza, J. 2008. "NeverEndingSearch." *School Library Journal.* http://www. schoollibraryjournal.com/blogger/2694.html (accessed May 23, 2009).

Valkenburg, P. M., and J. Peter. 2007. "Online communication and adolescent well-being: Testing the stimulation versus the displacement hypothesis." *Journal of Computer-Mediated Communication* 12 (4). http://jcmc.indiana.edu/vol12/issue4/valkenburg.html (accessed May 23, 2009).

Willard, N. (2007). *Cyber-Safe Kids, Cyber-Savvy Teens: Helping Young People Learn to use the Internet Safely and Responsibly.* San Francisco: Jossey-Bass.

Willard, N., and K. Steiner. 2007. *Cyberbullying and Cyberthreats: Responding to the Challenge of Online Social Aggression, Threats, and Distress.* Champaign, IL: Research Press.

Willis, J. 2006. *Research-Based Strategies to Ignite Student Learning.* Alexandria, VA: Association for Supervision and Curriculum Development.

Young Adult Library Services Association. 2006. *Social Networking and DOPA.* http://www.leonline.com/yalsa/positive_uses.pdf (accessed May 23, 2009).

INDEX

ABOUT THE EDITOR
AND CONTRIBUTORS

ABOUT THE EDITOR

Photo by Paul Rodriguez

ROBYN M. LUPA is Head of Children's Information Services at the Arvada Library of the Jefferson County Public Library. She is active in and presents workshops at both local and national professional organizations, as well as in ALA's YALSA division, including the Selected DVDs and Videos for Young Adults Committee, the Teen Web Site Advisory Committee, Outstanding Books for the College Bound, and the President's Program Planning Committee.

ABOUT THE CONTRIBUTORS

LINDA W. BRAUN is an Educational Technology Consultant for LEO: Librarians & Educators Online and an adjunct faculty member for Simmons College Graduate School of Library and Information Science. She works with schools, libraries, and other educational institutions to help them determine how to integrate and use technology effectively. From

2006 to 2009 she served as Blog Manager for the Young Adult Library Services Association (YALSA) and in 2009 she began a one-year term as President of the organization.

KELLY CZARNECKI is the Technology Education Librarian at the Public Library of Charlotte and Mecklenburg County's ImaginOn: the Joe and Joan Martin Center, a partnership with the Children's Theatre of Charlotte. She was the chair of the Technology for Young Adults Committee for YALSA. Kelly was chosen by *Library Journal* as a Mover & Shaker in 2007. She writes the Gaming Life Column for *School Library Journal.*

ERIN DOWNEY HOWERTON, MA, MLIS, is the School Liaison at the Johnson County Library in Overland Park, Kansas. Howerton has worked with youth for nearly a decade in both library and higher educational settings. She has published various articles and book chapters about library collections, intellectual freedom, and technology topics concerning youth. She is an active member of YALSA, having served on the Margaret A. Edwards Award committee and the Selected DVDs and Videos for Young Adults Committee, among others. She currently chairs the 2009 YALSA Preconference Committee and blogs about education, libraries, and technology at http://www.schoolingdotus.blogspot.com.

DAVE MOYER, currently a high school student, is the founder and president of Bitwire Media, a digital media company that produces blogs, podcasts, and other content on and offline. In addition, he writes for a myriad of Web sites and blogs around the web, primarily covering technology. Dave is also fairly active in historic preservation and has been involved with and spoken at many conferences and summits related to those issues. His personal Web site and blog can be found at http://davemoyer.org.

JENNA OBEE is the young adult information services librarian at the Standley Lake Library of the Jefferson County Public Library in Colorado. She is active in teen librarianship, including serving on the Colorado Teen Literature Conference committee and the Blue Spruce Young Adult Book Award committee.

MICHELLE PEARSON is a social studies teacher at Hulstrom Options School in the Adams 12 school district. She is the recipient of several fellowships that have focused on the design of primary source lessons, from NEH, the White House Historical Association, and the National Consortium of Teaching Asia. She was recognized as the 2007 Colorado Technology

Teacher of the Year and the 2008 Elgin Heinz Award Winner in Humanities, and she received a Colorado State Honors Award for excellence in historic preservation in 2008.

ANDREW WILSON is a Digital Producer at the New York Public Library. A graduate of Lafayette College and the library school at the University of South Florida, he began working at NYPL in 1987 as a children's librarian. He received a *New York Times* Librarian Award for his work with the Connecting Libraries and Schools Program in 2003. Along with the Brooklyn Public Library and Queens Library, he currently works on the development of the homework help site http://homeworkNYC.org and its related widgets. The site was named an Official Honoree of the 2006 Webby Awards.